A Vision to Win

"Harnessing the power of your imagination"

JAN MUIR

Copyright © 2017 Jan Muir : I BELIEVE I ACHIEVE

All rights reserved.

ISBN: 978-9874011-4-4 - E-Book E-Pub
ISBN: 978-0-9874011-3-7 - Printed
ISBN-13:
Self-Publishing via Ingram Spark
Graphic Artist Design – Rob W

A Vision to WIN
© Jan Muir 2017
All rights reserved. No Part of this publication may be reproduced, stored in a retrieval system, or transmitted in any form or by any means, electronic, mechanical, photocopying, recording or otherwise, without the prior written permission of the author.

This book is designed to provide information and motivation to our readers. It is sold with the understanding that the publisher is not engaged to render any type of psychological, legal, or any other kind of professional advice. The content of this publication is the sole expression and opinion of its author. No warranties or guarantees are expressed or implied by the author or publisher's choice to include any of the content in this volume. Neither the publisher nor the individual author(s) shall be liable for any physical, psychological, emotional, financial, or commercial damages, including, but not limited to special incidental consequential or other damages. Our views and rights are the same: You are responsible for your own choices and actions and results.

National Library Of Australia Cataloguing-in-Publication (pbk)

Author:	Muir, Jan, author
Title:	Vision to WIN / Jan Mur.
ISBN:	9780987401137 (paperback))
ISBN:	978-9874011-4-4 - E-Book; E-Pub
Subjects:	Visualization.
	Imagination.
	Mind and body.
	Imagery (Psychology)

Published by Jan Muir   Self-Published I Believe I Achieve

DEDICATION

This book is dedicated to my grand children

Rhys and Luke

To My Parents, Jim, Irene who gave me the opportunity to experience the sport of Athletics, I thank you so much for the opportunity to reach a goal once I knew it was achievable. Your involvement in the club management of Little Athletics in Wonthaggi; Victoria is commendable and being Marshall's in the regional/state team events of competition was an internal inspiration to me, I always admired my dad to stand tall and say

TAKE YOUR MARKS….. SE…T   THEN BANG THE GUN GOES OFF.

Thank you Mum and Dad

ENDORSEMENTS

Sheila Kennedy, Packenham; Victoria
I had the pleasure of meeting the wonderful Jan Muir in the earlier part of 2015 and it is a meeting that I will never forget. In Jan's new book Vision to WIN she speaks about a Magical Spirit and it was my own spiritual higher self or 'Magical Spirit' that guided me to introduce myself to Jan.

Sometimes we know without knowing and in that knowing whether it be 'reason, season or lifetime we connect with another person on a 'higher level' as Jan calls it 'Very Important Magic'.

Jan 'gifted' me the opportunity to read her manuscript and I felt both honoured and blessed. An Authors work is precious indeed and releasing it to the hands thoughts and feelings of another is an enormous step.

As someone who communicates with my own Magical Spirit as Jan does with hers, it was at 4am on October 23rd 2016 that I received an insistent message. I had been reading Jan's Manuscript before I went to bed.

Rather than attempt to explain it to you I will share what I wrote to Jan later that morning.

Hi Jan, I have been reading your book, slowly so as to absorb it and around 4 am I was lying awake in the dark as I often do and your name came into my mind.
I will share what came next;

A woman strong who speaks her truth
Shadowed souls in need of proof
And so, the journey does begin
Guided as you go within.

I got up to write the message down then a few moments later the message continued.

A guide, a mentor, a friend.

Jan takes your hand and walks with you on a journey into discovery.

Awakening your own inner knowing.

The gift that never grows old.

I could not say it better myself.

May you enjoy the blessings of your journey with Jan as I have.

With much love

Sheila Kennedy
www.sheila-kennedy.com
www.soundsfromsource.com
www.soundsfromsourceacademy.com
www.energeticbalanceandharmony.com
http://amazon.com/author/sheila-kennedy
Revolution Radio@Freedomslips.com and Welcome to the 1% with Sheila Kennedy

☙☙☙

Anne Aleckson, Brisbane
A Vision to Win is an insight into the mind of a young athlete using her innate ability to receive guidance from deep within, sometimes referred to as the Higher Self. I've used this connection to create my own business and community by following the inner voice to help me

achieve more.

We all have the ability to connect with this part of ourselves and Vision to Win gives you a very simple outline of the conversations you could be having that will help you stretch for your desired outcome and achieve anything you set your mind to.

Anne Aleckson
www.AnneAleckson.com
https://www.facebook.com/anne.aleckson

Julie Ortiz; Grammar Editor,
   "As humans, one of our major desires is the desire to be successful and to feel that we've been able to use our gifts in the best way that we can. Unfortunately, there are many people today who do not even realize that they have one gift or the other, and subsequently they live their lives struggling with mediocrity. In this book, the author, Jan Muir, offers insights which have been tried and tested in her life from adolescence right up till this very moment.

Through her personal encounters, Jan reveals how she was able to record success in athletics competitions as an adolescent and remain strong throughout the challenges she faced. In this book, you'll find the keys to unlocking your innate potential and quenching every doubt that may arise in your heart. With the right attitude, this book will surely change your life for the better. You can be better than you already are, you can be the person of your dreams. As they say, second place is great, but the winner gets gold! Are you ready to win?"

Lisa Syme, NSW
Finally finished your book. Wow!

It teaches me a lot about you as a person. It teaches me a lot about your spirit and your mental strength.
Well done and good on you for sharing those intimate parts of your life, for laying out to bare for everyone to read. This book taught me a lot. A great book for all to read parents and teenagers

ಸಿಸಿಸಿ

Johaan Kaa, Brisbane
A Vision to Win really shares a story that is unique to us all, however not all of us realise its strength. Jan takes us on a journey and allows us to realise that the voice chatter we hear is an indication of what we can look forward to achieve; both in the positive and negative thoughts you have. You won't be disappointed in reading this book.

- Johaan Kaa;- Brisbane
Entrepreneur, Business Owner, Speaker
http://fromsepsis2success.com/
https://www.facebook.com/johaan.kaa

ಸಿಸಿಸಿ

Trish Springsteen, Brisbane

Jan's book Vision to Win, appeals to both the young and adult reader. It shows the young reader that they have ability to use the strength of the mind to focus on achieving the goals they are aiming for.
For the adult reader, it brings clarity in realising that the

signposts are always there; nothing is happening to us for no reason, it's our perceptions and mind set (positive and negative) that takes us off the path.

Jan shares a way to connect to the inner chatter and to find strength in all that is happening to you.

Jan has built on her own unique experience as a child where she harnessed her inner voice and mind set to achieve her goals in her athletic career. It was not until years later Jan realised that what she took for granted as a child is something many of us young and old have forgotten or don't know how to connect and use.

I have worked with Jan for a while now and I know the passion and tenacity that lies within this lady. We are all on a journey and what this book shares with you is the experience that we all have and the potential that is there if we only reach out grab it and use it.

This is a book with a powerful message that you can take, connect with and use.

Well worth the read!!

Trish Springsteen
Multi International Award Winning Speaker Mentor Coach Author
https://www.facebook.com/trishspringsteenspeaking/
http://trischel.com.au/about-us

FORWARD

Stephen and I met Jan through a networking contact and over a coffee discussed her experiences and goals. What struck both of us was her passion and determination, which inspired me to want to be part of her journey. This was around September 2013 and we have never looked back.

Jan's journey with me was one of learning that we gave each other. Jan was passionate about her stories that she wanted to share, and I became eager to work with her. We worked seamlessly to eventually find the writing style that brought the best out in Jan's storytelling. With every hurdle, she was relentless and never gave up. When times were hard she persisted, following her own advice to believe and achieve.

I have never met anyone with so much determination, energy and belief. Knowing the adversity, she has faced in life and seeing her confront and beat some of those personal demons gives Jan all the authority to write and share her experiences in the way that she does. Not only do I feel blessed being a part of this journey but in also having gained a valued friend in both Jan and Vito.

Kerrie Butler
Bachelor Behavioural Studies

"Inspiration"
Find Your Future Here
Jane Powell

"You hold your future in your mind."
Let your mind flow freely for a moment.
Look into the future and imagine that you have no limitations on what you can be, have or do. Imagine that you have everything you need to get there.

Time, money, people, smarts are all readily available.

What do you see?

Your future vision is an imaginary creation of your ideal life, and this vision flows from your most important values. It idealizes both who you are and who you can become.

Let your vision crystallize so clearly that you can almost touch it.
Let yourself feel the emotion that comes with imaging your ideal life.
Once you do, you'll be amazed. The steps you need to take to turn your vision into reality will crystallize, too.

For, this is your pathway to an ideal future.

CONTENTS

       Dedication

       Endorsement

       Forward

       Inspiration

001	Preface	Pg 1
002	How this Book is your Guide	Pg 11
003	In the beginning	Pg 16
1	Getting to the Starting Line	Pg 29
2	Connecting with Spirit	Pg 37
3	Training Sessions	Pg 47
4	Reflection of Your Ability	Pg 55
5	Visualisation to Reality	Pg 62
6	People project their Thoughts and Feelings all around You	Pg 66
7	Tall Poppy	Pg 69

8	Positive Self-Talk Tough Competition	Pg 73
9	Perfecting your Technique – Flying Starts How to see it already achieved	Pg 81
10	Being part of a team -Relay races… You can't Visualise for Anyone else only for Self	Pg 96
11	Crossing the Finish Line	Pg 102
12	Who is Magical Spirit	Pg 108
	Bio About Author	Pg 114
	Journal your thoughts as your read	Pg 116

001 **PREFACE**

As you start reading the beginning of this article, you may find yourself pondering "Why this book?" Why any book for that matter? This book has crossed your path for several reasons. Any book you hold has a reason or a message to share with you. Some of the content of this book may reach you and touch you, while the essence of some other books may be to share a story of heart from actual events. Each book has a specific message for you.

Every author's aim is to have you read their book and take something from the book to improve your life or give you a good feeling about something you may like to experience. This book is no different to the next. As the author, my aim is to bring about awareness in the power of the mind and the imagination on the screen of your mind.

Imagine what it would be like if you could find your passion, your drive on something you would like to achieve in life. This book can assist you with understanding the ways in which you can use the power of the mind to bring the result you would like to achieve for yourself into practice.

Is it easy? No, it's not.

Is it possible? YES, it is.

Will you have to do things differently? Possibly.

You probably already know what I'm about to share and that's OK. In those early years of my existence I witnessed what I was doing as a young 10-year-old that later in life proved to be the biggest ahh haaa! I could have ever known in life. I was using my mind power so efficiently I had no idea I was doing it and it felt so right. I never shared with anyone in life because I was afraid I would be laughed at, even be told I was being silly. Fifty years ago, no one spoke about the power of the mind, and if you did you were most likely a scientist who understood more than a young ten years old girl. I never shared with any one; I was too afraid and too scared and thought I wouldn't be listened to.

At ten years of age I did not know it then like I understand it now. How could I, nobody talked about the mind and its incredible power of bringing something to us all. How each of us sees something for our own good and most do not take notice of and do something with towards our goals.

There are some groups of us that do go on to win gold medals at Olympics or climb mountains of great height or reach high potentials in a company or invent something new and ingenious.

The most powerful message is there for us all, all we have to do is connect and gain trust and build clarity around what that is for YOU. This book's message is a diamond, however large or small it is what resonates for you in this message. You can use it to improve on your life in some way.

As you read every word of this book you will feel a sense of clarification, gain understanding and more knowledge towards your end goal. This book is designed to inspire you more and improve aspects of your personal development outlook.

You probably know all that you know, from all your experiences, however there will always be something more to learn from the message written within. This was what the author learnt about forty years after she had used visualisation in her young life. We will get to that word 'visualisation' in a minute.

I also learnt about the strength of the mind and what it is capable of, something that I really wished I had known at the young age of ten. My life would no doubt have been different if I had known this much earlier in life. I've not lived an unhappy life, on the contrary, I've lived an adventurous life, and I've had overcome some challenges along the way. However, despite all this, it has been the understanding of the mind and its strength that has had the biggest impact on me. The incredible thing is that while it was unknown to me then, today I've realised I was using the mind function correctly all those years at ten years of age. Maybe you are using them too and are not aware of what is occurring right now. It is not something that is taught in schools with great understanding, in fact it is only now that we are starting to know more about the mind and its incredible power. Nonetheless, this knowledge can help us to make a huge change in our life.

What I did not know was the understanding of the strength of the mind and its intuitive direction that was an indication for my journey. And it is the same for you as well – choosing to learn to understand and become aware of the strength of the mind's ability is the key.

Your mind is one of the most powerful computers in the world and everyone has one - a mind that is!

Everyone is born with a very special gift; however, some never turn on the power, some baulk at it, and some never even want to believe it is a true indication of where your life could go.

Our mind is a very strong tool and some people are clever and utilize its strengths in specific fields, while others have no idea how to even tap into it and identify what they could do, if even to approach a simple exercise in a different way. There is always a better way to do most things in life. It is not always the way you have chosen.

Let's go back to that word 'visualization', what does this mean –

Visualize:

1. To form a mental image of; envisage: tried to visualize the scene as it was described.
2. To make visible.
3. To form a mental image.

4. To make perceptible to the mind or imagination.
5. Using a psychology perspective:-
   to form a mental image of (something incapable of being viewed or not at that moment visible)
6. A medical perspective:-
   to view by means of an X-ray the outline of (a bodily organ, structure, or part), to recall or form mental images or pictures.

For the purpose of this book we will use the 5th description; to form a mental image of something incapable of being viewed or not at that moment visible. As a young ten years, old child, I had no idea, neither was I able to understand the power of the mind, nevertheless, I could apply it efficiently and thus I could gain high success in sport as a child. I didn't understand at that time that this was normal, it wasn't until forty-five years later before I realised this. What I'm trying to share with you is information that will awaken your mind cells to this powerful part of your brain so that you may be able to use it wisely for your own success, such as to gain better grades in school, to work towards the career you wish to pursue, or to be that budding entrepreneur and make a mark in life. In a nutshell, the information contained in this book will help you to be recognised in your field.

The events that appear in this book happened to me, and I hope you can join me to use these strategies for your life as well. Instructions will be as practical as possible; however, it will mean you may need to apply some concentration to exercise this part of your brain as you move through this book. At different points, there will be support with some Pearls of Wisdom known as POW's. These can be pointers of awareness throughout the book and there may be a conscious effort for you to take some positive action using these POW's.

Before we jump into the heart of the book let's look at Jan's story. Once upon a time... This is no fairy tale, nor is it a fabrication of experiences. Jan's story is unique and varied and everyone travels through life learning as they go - well we would hope that they do. The author wishes no harm to any one reading or to say your life will be the same - because it won't, however, similar experiences may occur at some point in time, or you may know of someone whom you can relate as we move through.

No matter where you are in life – either as a young adult or a mature adult, I know that what I am sharing with you in this book can and will have an impact on your life... as soon as you implement the exercises shared with you.

I grew up in country Victoria and had a good childhood and loving parents who always inspired my two sisters and I to be involved in sport. There were no technical implements as available today to utilise in any quiet moment. All three children had jobs to do in helping on the family farm; growing up in the country area about 100km south of Melbourne this really had you appreciate life in a totally different way.

I moved through junior school, never being an extremely academic person; always trying my best and getting average grades, however, it was at sport that I excelled the most. There were numerous opportunities to play netball and to participate in gymnasium (until the club closed due to insufficient interest), and I learned to swim at a young age. In my senior school years, I played squash, and most of all competed in athletics all through my young life. As life then moved on into my adult years, I was always involved in sport in some way; even participating as an aerobics instructor when the craze first started. I continued doing this for about 5 years.

My story took a small impacting swing when my daughter's father was diagnosed with Alzheimer's dementia, and I sought to know why this disease was occurring. Unbeknown to me, I was about to learn so many aspects of the mind and its power and strength. Since my childhood days I knew I had a gift, however, this was the time to follow it through.

At this point in time I was living in Darwin and had been for several years. I had had the opportunity to travel a lot of Australia with my then partner and with his failing health I was forced to place him in a home. He passed on a few years later. With my daughter keen to start again, we decided to move to Brisbane. We had spent only a short number of years in Brisbane before I was diagnosed with breast cancer and found myself facing my own adversities and struggles for life. Part of that experience made me look harder into the power of the mind to understand the strength of what gift I had been given. The power and strength of the mind. We all have this same gift. Unfortunately, I just did not know it nor understand at that time how to use its strength.
Your mind power is a gift, and by reading this book I hope you will be able to harness its strength even more and be more aware of its strength and learn from the experience ahead of me.

Eight years after getting my health back, and after thirty-three years in public service I was made redundant. I had started my career in the Northern Territory, and despite having moved interstate I could pick up my career in the same arena. This impacted on my life in a very new way - being without a steady income and now 55 years of age really opened a new door for me.

I came to recall I had made a firm decision earlier in life about when to retire. My decision then was to retire at the age of fifty-five. This decision was made when I was about twenty-five years old. I remembered thinking "years from now everything will be OK and safe and nothing will happen to me". This was the thought that filled my mind then. Now, at fifty-five years and seventeen days, I was redundant from a very secure job. The power of the mind is stronger than we give it credit for. Be very careful what you wish for in all areas of life. Your mind can bring this to you, and understanding how this works is the key to your success.

My story is about helping you to become aware of the strength of your mind power and to gain an awareness and understanding that everything you see for yourself is achievable for you. We can call this visioning using your mind's eye. The principal aim of this book is to share this information with adults; young and old, and to assist them to understand this knowledge so that they can apply it in their own lives.

Anyone can do this. I want to help you reach your goal. I'm the first to accept that, that is a bold statement. However, nonetheless, I also know that it is possible once you have an understanding and learn some of the techniques and engage the brain you will be able to apply it to any areas of your life.

Imagine what it would be like if you could appreciate how powerful your mind really is and begin to apply this to your school work, your career, your relationships, in fact anywhere you want to apply it to improve your life. It's all up to you, you have a choice and it's OK whatever your choice is. How you visualise any situation in life is an indication of the positive or negative outcome. Gaining understanding on this in the positive can be of great help to your life.

Appreciating how you are taught to do things, and then using the visualising technique I'll share with you, you will be able to apply it to all areas of your life. In learning this, you will come to understand the conscious and subconscious mind more and then apply the visualising techniques. You are sure to get great results with this technique.

The truth is this, 90% of your habits are held in your subconscious. Learning to train your brain in a way that you trick your mind with visualising will improve your life, I'm certain of that. Visualising and forcing the mind is not a way to your success. It's also every action step you take along the path doing one thing every day towards that outcome.

It's also more of knowing a way to master your mind, and this is a process.

As with every aspect of life, there is the first stage that we learn, if that does not feel right then we can unlearn those things that do not serve us well. After some time and exploration, we can learn better ways to do things and improve things in our life to reach our fullest potential and outcomes.

My outcome at a young age was to win a Gold Medal in Athletics.

002 *HOW THIS BOOK IS YOUR GUIDE*

My approach to my athletic journey at a very young age was unique on many levels – whilst I do not want to write a biography, I wanted to share my wisdom and awareness so you can learn and apply this in your own life. I will call this awareness '**Pearls of Wisdom'** (also known a **POW** throughout the book) and I share the insights as you read through.

Let's start with introducing you to a list of **POW's** .

Magic Spirit was the first clarity that I realised later in life. Part of life's journey in trusting my inner ability and listening to myself and the mind chatter that occurred. In today's language, we have come to know this as listening to our higher self. I'll call this my Spiritual self, my higher self, which is sometimes known as the inner guidance. It is also having a knowing inside of me that I know what I need to know and then I go out and do it. Everyone has a spiritual self and is guided by this throughout their lifetime.

Magical Spirit as called throughout the book is a part of life every day and we are often not in tune with it when it's the biggest guide to have in life.

My ***Spiritual*** side is forever guiding me and sharing information from all aspects of the body that I am in tune with. I sincerely hope that you can connect to this part of yourself during the story.

Heart – this will always be as we feel in our heart. It is a knowing that I knew what I was doing was right for me. I follow every action through to reach a result. Knowing what it is that I need to know, I am guided to improve on this and I know it will be right for my outcome. I act to get the right information to move forward. Everything that is achieved is done with ease and in alignment.

Intuition – this is an inner voice that is always talking inside of me, and sharing guidance or instruction on how I can do things. My intuition works closely with my heart and 3rd Eye Perception and is totally aware when doubt is endeavouring to take me off path. We all know when this occurs – our moods or attitude may change, or even positive energy may change to negative energy. We feel uneasy with what is occurring around us.

3rd Eye Perception is a key area of your imagination. In other words, it can be referred to as your visualisation. The 3rd Eye is a strong element and has a strong connection to the intellect, heart and Magic Spirit.

Visualisation is what is true for you. If you can see it in

your mind's eye, then it is achievable for you. We are not taught this and how to use this part of the brain. Science is starting to really get a better understanding of how this works. However, it has always been part of each of us. As Napoleon Hill said back in 1937,

> *"Whatever the mind can conceive it can achieve."*

Your **Expression** through your **Voice** is another area of connection; to share a thought or a feeling of what you feel or maybe thinking. Expression through voice connects us together in ways so unique. For example, some of us have a singing voice and create beautiful music that resonates to us on different levels. Others have a voice to speak out and show a way at presentations. Even your teachers at school have a voice, they lead you and teach you things from different points of education.

Earth is what we ground ourselves back to. We can become centred and this helps with a good balance for our overall systems. Being grounded can have a positive or negative effect. However, most of the time when we are in flow[1] being grounded can have a positive effect. Sometimes we have a negative outlook and that is ok, as we can have a down day every so often. This is generally the time we can let things go and start from a grounded base. To be grounded you could be in bare feet on the lush grass, or letting the waves roll over your feet as you sink

---

[1] Being in flow is when everything we are doing is for the positive result, we keep doing and nothing seems to be in our way. Everything flows with ease and direction.

into the sand whilst at the beach. Maybe you are climbing a tree and just want to feel a part of it, you feel complete with it, or maybe you are hiking in the rain forest and you stand still in the stillness of the forest. Everyone has a way of feeling grounded. Everyone will know what that is for them and return to it often to feel grounded each time.

Body is the vehicle that holds us together. The intellect is part of the body; the heart is part of the body as is the 3rd Eye. Expression of voice resonates within the body and our being is the Spiritual body. Earth connects to the body; in a way, we are on a grounded platform. Connection to the earth is in many forms via the sea, rivers, forests, mountains, and plants. Our home is where we can be grounded. Whatever it is for you, it is the place where you feel those feelings of peace within you.

The **body** is the instrument that brings this all together and we are responsible to keep the body healthy, happy and flowing all the time.

There are two things to be very clear on that connect this all together as Deepak Chopra explains in his book *'Fire in the Heart'*.

"Energy vibrates everywhere in the universe.

Spirituality is about a new way of seeing and a new way of being.

There is an invisible something to be discovered inside all of us.

It's a mysterious force holding things together and making patters out of the clouds of energy."

What I aim to share here is each of these points weave into the story as lessons at the end of each chapter and I advise you to see if you can gain the connection for yourself. As you move through each chapter, it doesn't matter if you are not able to connect as we are all on different paths and the vibrational match for some will need to be learned, while for others it will be ready to witness. Whatever you gain for you is right for you and that is all that matters. Be open to receive and more will come.

…. Let's move on to find out what that source could be.

003   *IN THE BEGINNING*

Are you an achiever?

What does that mean? Well, for me it was a knowing inside of me that if I put my mind to anything I can achieve it. An achiever is one who acts towards the end goal. You know inside that it is something you want to achieve as a way of gaining momentum towards a bigger goal.

If you knew how to reach for your dream and goals would you go for it?

This could mean many things; such as how hard are you going to work towards your result doing one thing every day towards that end goal? You know you can do anything to achieve, so in taking specific steps towards that result you can start to see your dream emerge. Every day is a new day. Encouragement is shared to do one thing every day towards the result and you will reach it faster than you realise. Keep stretching.

Do you want to aim higher?
Do you want to be more successful in your life?

Double edged questions. Do you want to aim high? Do you want to be more successful in your life? Of course, you do. The answer is in the question.

Did you answer yes? Or did you shy away from making a commitment to do this? We all want to aim high and we all want to be successful in our lives. To each of us that means something different. For the point of alignment with this book, I wanted to win a gold medal; I wanted to stand on the dais[2] at the end of the race with the gold medal around my neck. My aiming high was to win, my wanting to be successful was in being with the gold medal I had won.

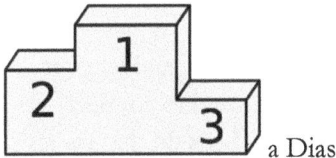
a Dias

How dedicated are you to your goal?

Dedication is a strong word and means "the quality of being dedicated or committed to a task or purpose. For example, "his dedication to his duties". When you have a greater understanding of words you can bring them to mean more to you. Now let's ask the question again.

---

[2] Dias is a small stand that represents first; second and third in an event, it's a place to stand to be presented with medals or trophies after an athletic event. It is also known as a podium. For the purpose of this book I only ever knew it as standing on the Dias.

How dedicated are you to your goal? I hope you could say with a strong knowing inside of you that you want to achieve this goal (whatever that goal is for you) and that you will do everything you can towards that goal to reach it with success and in a good time line. You will stay committed and you will give it time to grow as you improve every day.

Despite these questions being open-ended, regardless of your answers at this point, the truth of them all is that to get to the top of any achievement, dedication is required.

Having the ability to feel the emotions attached to your dreams also has you on first base towards your goal. Having a better understanding of what your dream is, looks like and feels like to you is also a great starting point.

At this very moment sit quietly for a minute and let your imagination swim in the flow of your mind to connect with what your goal is. There you go! Let's do that for a minute or two.
Remember to breathe slowly in and out with long deep breaths. Note anything that comes up for you on paper. What were you visualising in terms of your dreams? How are you using your imagination?

Visualising your dreams and what you want to achieve in life begins with a single thought. Another thought will be added to this original thought, turning your single thought into an idea. It is prudent to note here that thought is everywhere, every day. In a single day, we all have thousands of thoughts; however, it is important to note that not all of them are relevant to your end goal.

It is important to recognise that we are all having thoughts. The thoughts that you connect to with a feeling or a knowing is an important thought.

The thought can consist of many things. What a thought consists of varies for each person. A few examples could be:

- getting better school results, - reaching top of the class
- getting top marks for a project you must complete, - a scientist connects all their experiments to the result to get an outcome.
- achieving great marks for a music lesson, - being able to reach that high note for your song you want to sing, or instrument to play
- being selected for the cricket or football team, - represent yourself in an Australian team
- attending driving school to obtain your driver's licence for the first time.

The list is endless. Rare thinking people already know this.

Did you notice what it was like the day you stepped onto the athletics track? You may have been 5 or you may have been older.

Can you remember what that felt like?

Could you see yourself winning a gold medal for the event you were about to compete in? Little by little you can place yourself within your own example. However, I am going to use the example of an athlete wanting to win a gold medal. Whatever is relevant for you and your goal is important at this point in time.

When a thought occurs to you that you want to achieve something, you may hear a voice in your brilliant mind asks

"Is that really what you want?"

You will sit and often ponder on that thought for a day or in some cases it could be a week or even longer if you are a procrastinator, often not knowing where this idea could lead you. However, it is important to just allow the thought to dance in your mind and twist and turn on every excuse you can think of or you could be excitedly jumping, thinking you can achieve your end goal. What happened to me was an experience that really did not make any sense at the time, all I knew inside of me was this chatter as I listened to this voice, unaware of the connection and where it would take me.

I stepped onto the athletics track and the chatter in my mind started with a faraway spiritual voice whispering in my ear and I heard the words "You can achieve it." My immediate thought is it's possible. You can be successful, it will take dedication and it will take you to aim high. Yes, it is all possible, this little voice whispers inside of me, and it is for you as well. Sit quietly and ponder on those thoughts, listen to the voice speaking to you from within your mind.

Take a moment to imagine you are standing on the edge of the athletic track. The voice then whispers again "the thought you are having is yours, if you really want it? It's yours if you are prepared to do the hard yards. You can stand on the dais[2] and receive the gold medal you want".

As you look around; you find nobody is physically there to touch, however, you have a mental image of a magical spirit being present, looking at you, and talking to you. He is just like any other person, only he is clothed all in purple. For the purpose of this book, this guide represents 'Spirit'. Spirit can be seen through your own eyes; nobody else can see your spirit, you cannot touch him, however you know he is there. Imagine he is dressed in purple clothing with gold trim, he looks amazing. He is standing in a foggy mirage with beautiful eyes looking at you.

Magical Spirit asks you the question, "Do you really want to run on the athletics track and believe you are confident enough to win?"

You answer back with a firm "yes"; "Yes, I do want to run, I know I can run fast".

The words are not physically spoken or loud, they all occur in your head. This is called the inner voice. The magical spirit's image moves from left to right and asks

"What can you do to make this happen?"

"I am not sure", I say, continuing with "I want to win my race, I want to compete. I know I can run fast and I want to win".

Magical Spirit has moved again and is now coming from behind me, his voice is deep and resonates with me, he reaches out his arm to take my right hand.

He is now looking at me and says "If you allow me to take your right hand, I can give you a way to make this happen. Do you really want to do this?" A long pause with a very long sigh.

"Yes, I answered, turning to look directly at Magical Spirit's eyes. I want to win a gold medal. I want to be a champion runner".

Magical Spirit answers "Okay, I think I can see your interest is high and I can see you have a drive to succeed. Let's ask your visual side to show you a way".

"A way to what?" I ask, unsure as to what was the magical spirit talking about.

A way to show you…Magical Spirit cuts in saying… "I thought you wanted this to happen". "I do".

"Well, first you must trust in me as magical spirit will flow to you, and let it guide you to show you ways to reach your full potential" said Magical Spirit.

"Ahh… Okay" … "Can I trust you to show me a way?"

Magical Spirit replied with, "The real question is how do you see it and believe in it, do you believe that it is achievable?" This will be the way to show you that you can trust in me.

Magical Spirit says "I am going to guide you through an exercise to help you see the way, would you prefer to sit or laydown on this ground here?" I said I think I can trust you and I will lie on the ground.
Magical Spirit proceeded to say "I ask you to close your

eyes and trust that with each word I say it will assist you to learn something new. Now gently and slowly let your eyes close." I want you to feel the ground you will be running on, just let your body feel the earth as you lay there".

The magical Spirit asks. "Are you in a comfortable place?"

"Yes".

"Just listen to my voice, keep your eyes closed the whole time and see if you can see in your mind the words I share with you. When I am finished, I will ask you to share with me what you were able to see in your imagination or on the screen of your mind.

Magical Spirit repeated again in a softened voice "keep your eyes closed and only listen to my voice".

Magical Spirit begins to speak. His voice is deep and soft and he is hard to hear, yet I feel the words he says within me as he shares a description of the magic occurring on the race track. He doesn't use me as the model, he shares that of a young girl who has an ability to run, she can learn how to improve her technique so that she runs faster in practice. She can learn lots about her training hard and how to eat healthy to strengthen her bones and exercises to stay fit. He shares what to do when a training coach arrives in her life; listening to his advice and completing all the tasks he asks you to do. The coach will show you a way that will improve your running style. You will learn from this coach how to position yourself to get a flying start at every race. There will be a session on learning how to prepare for the race with a mental strength and focus, and the benefits of using a specific start called the crouch start.

There is some silence for a few moments and I feel a sense of being whispered to, "If you can see it on the screen of your mind, you can imagine it is happening; you can believe it to be true. Everything you conceive is achievable".

I lay motionless on the ground. I could hear what the Magical Spirit was saying. I could feel the excitement in my body when Magical Spirit spoke of winning the race and feeling so proud of my achievements. I just wanted to be soaked into this bath of words and inspiration, and the longer I sat in this space the clearer it became. I could sense there was some movement around me.

Magical Spirit kept moving around my motionless body. I was asked a couple of questions by Magical Spirit.

"Do you believe it is achievable?"

"Yes".

"Do you see any pictures on the screen of your mind?" asked Magical Spirit.

I was not sure how to answer at first; do I speak out loud or do I whisper all the words to myself? I chose to share with confidence and as I spoke the words flowed from my mouth.

"There are lots of children around at the same event I am at, and I run several events to qualify over time. I run first and second in these qualifying events. I make it to the state finals. I compete against other competitors, who are the best in their region. I win each event and I stand on the dais to receive a gold medal for my achievements".

"Ah" said Magical Spirit, "what does the gold medal feel like?"

I sense a feeling of pride as I felt tears run down my cheeks, my eyes staying closed during this very short conversation with Magical Spirit.

"It has a blue ribbon around it. The medal has wording of Victorian State Championships for Little Athletics. I see a gold medallion hanging from the blue ribbon. I am standing on the dais and I lean forward for the presentation of the officials placing the medal around my neck. There is some weight to it as it hangs on my chest. I actually feel proud and well up inside with joy in achieving the gold medal".

Magical Spirit now in a still place looking over my motionless body on the ground says "We have completed lesson one on your journey to achieve a gold medal. Your passion is evident through the tears on your cheeks. The trembling in your voice demonstrates the proud feeling you experience as you see yourself achieving your goal and feel the excitement from your efforts. What I now ask is that you carry this with you for the rest of your life. You will achieve this at some point in your life.

There will be hard yards; there will be some pain, not pain of losing just pain of pushing forward in the training to come. There will be elation to reach this height of achievement. There will be disappointment when you don't stay with focus, those are the lessons you will learn on this journey.

Magical Spirit softly whispers to me "you can now slowly open your eyes and stand up again. I have completed my first lesson". As I move to open my eyes and sit up I can still see the image of his gold tipped purple outfit. He is now standing right in front of me, his purple clothing with a shimmer of sparkle. I had not really seen the sparkle before, However, nevertheless, it was much clearer.

He looked directly into my eyes saying "It was all there for you. All you must do is to stay with the belief that it is achievable. Keep the vision of the dream alive on the screen of your mind and believe it will be achieved".

Magical Spirit moved to step back as if he was going. I wanted to reach out to him however, he was not able to be touched, I shouted "Don't go!", "How can I ever do this, I am only ten years old?"

Magical Spirit shares that "I will appear again when I hear you ask for me, or I see you reviewing this vision when you sit still and remember this experience".

"I am always here. It is being able to work with me and visualise me on the screen of your mind that is the hardest part. However, I will show up when you need me the most, I always do. I know there will be other thoughts and moments that will tug at you, and attempt to throw your focus and lead you away from your achievement. It is important to keep your vision strong through doing the exercise we have done today. Take the time to really focus on this moment. He took another step back and the purple Magical Spirit faded into the background. He was gone so quickly.

I looked all around me and felt sad at his departure. I couldn't see him anywhere; I couldn't see anything that resembled magical spirit. I was left standing on the edge of the athletics track.

Out of nowhere I hear my father's strong loud voice calling "Hey Jan what are you doing? It's time to go now, come on, hop into the car. We have to go home to milk the cows."

(Sole Note: There are many lessons ahead of you to absorb and learn. Therefore, it is okay if you read this book or the chapters therein over and over again. Repetition helps us absorb and learn. Go ahead, dive in and come back to read the information or do the exercises as many times as your heart desires.)

Pearls of Wisdom

- ☺ I witnessed Magic Spirit with the voices in my head.
- ☺ I used the imagination (3rd eye perception) with the image I could see.
- ☺ I felt it in my heart I had a knowing I would win.
- ☺ I listened to the voices sharing words of wisdom to me and I expressed it in my voice with talking to myself that I could do this.
- ☺ Standing on the athletics track, the vibration I felt was so deep inside my body.
- ☺ I always feel connected to earth when on the track.

Chapter 1

GETTING TO THE STARTING LINE

Mum and Dad took care of the cows on our county farm in Victoria. There other jobs to be taken care of on the farm, such as feeding the animals, collecting eggs and milking the many cows. Everyone helped as it was a family affair. Mum and Dad also ensured that we three girls were involved in some type of sport such as tennis, netball, and squash, in addition to my passion for athletics.

Out of the many sports we participated in as a family, it was athletics that became a passion for the whole family. Dad was president of our local club for several years. He also held the position of a starter at the Regional and State Championships.

I fondly remember him shouting "Take your marks", he was a good starter of the races.

Athletes moved to the starting line, sometimes in a standing start or to position themselves on the blocks in the crouch position. When everyone was settled and quiet you would hear a soft however, yet firm "Set", ring from the starter's voice– then Bang! the cap gun would go off and the race was underway.

Whenever I was on the starting line and dad was an official starter for the day he would always step back and let another official starter get the race on its way. He ensured this occurred even when he was the Chief Starter at the state finals events.

Mum also had a very active role in the athletic club we were part of, along with several other active parents. One of her roles was to manage the individual local teams. This took several mums, all working together, while some of the dads were officials on the ground. Many kids had to be organised into specific groups and taken to allocated marshalling area for their events and making sure each child was on time for the marshalling officials.

My parents were also involved with the training sessions at the local club for children who wanted to enhance their running style or improve on a jump they were attempting. This could be the high jump, long jump, or even triple jump. It was a huge effort for the whole family, especially when most of the training occurred in the evenings when the milking on the farm needed to be done. Thus, mum generally completed the milking that had to be done, whilst dad drove us girls to the training events.

Even though I helped on the farm and in other activities, it was my love of athletics that really had my focus. Much of my concentration was on running. My athletic days started as a sport activity that occurred on the school grounds.

Most kids can relate to athletics, as it is one of the most common areas that all kids had to compete in at some point during their schooling years. Age events at primary school were conducted in the school, then to the regional finals or even through to state finals. At high school the education has physical education in which athletics is included and you are expected to participate as part of the overall assessment.

The school was divided into teams and each team would then compete against the others to determine who would be selected to represent the school in that age event against the local schools. The team colours were red, blue, green and yellow. My primary school colour was red and I was in the blue team.

As a young child, I always wanted to run and have fun, and as the years rolled on more and more competitiveness occurred in each age group. I was challenged numerous times for the 100 meters or even the 70 meters' events. Each time I was challenged, I always knew I could win. I just felt a certain feeling inside that had me feel like I was a bolt of lightning and the flash was the race; it always seemed to go so fast.

One day whilst I was standing before the starting line of my first official running event, for the school district event I started to question myself "how fast can I really go?" I felt something whisper in my ear that faraway magical spirit was talking to me again – "as fast as you want to go" he said, I felt excited. I then heard the little quiet voice whisper again, "However fast you really want to go, if you want to come first place, then you have to run fast".

This little voice seemed to be very close as if it was inside of me.

As I stood quietly till I heard my name being called by the official then I moved to the next lane allocation to stand in front of the starting line. I was now moving towards running my first race in my age group. I was about 8-10 years of age. I moved slowly to the line. I felt a little flutter in my tummy. Was it nerves? Or was it more a feeling of pure excitement to be here? There was no time to work out the meaning of what I was feeling. I just knew I had to run fast.

There was complete silence and stillness amongst all the runners waiting behind the starting line before the senior teacher called "Take your marks!", then "Set!" was said by the starter. There was a second starter on the other side of the track watching for any movement in the competitors. It was an anxious moment waiting for the starter's gun to go off.

There was a bang and then a second bang, indicating that someone has moved before the official gun went off so everyone was called back to the starting line.

"False start" called the voice from the side line, one of the lanes had broken and left the starting line before the actual gun had gone off. Everyone had to return to behind the starting line and reposition themselves again. It caused for more activity in my tummy, only this time I knew it was nerves. I was nervous and thankful it was not me that had left the starting line before the gun had gone. As the athletes were again called to the line the little voice in my ear appeared to whisper again.

Magical Spirit whispered "Breathe deep, slow down your breathing you will need every breath to get to the end. Slow and steady wins the race, you can do this." I took a deep breath in and listened to the starter's instructions.

"Take your marks" called the starter again, the girl that broke was given a warning that her next break would cause her to be eliminated from the event. I knew I had heard Magical Spirit whisper to me. I felt his presence yet I could not see him. I moved slowly to the starting line, staying as nimble as I could; I needed to be ready and relaxed in my body and not feel any tension in my muscles.

I was about to get into position, to restart the race. This time there was a different silence around us, nobody moved and it was oh so quiet. The starter's voice says "Se…tt", with a long pause between the 'e' and the 't'.

Competitors moved to be in the best place waiting for the gun to go off, ready to push off hard. It all happened so quickly and seconds later, BANG! the gun had gone off and the race was on its way.

Our lanes were marked out in a twine draping the full '70 meters' of the race, which extended to '100 meters' for other events. The finish line had a white tape stretched from one lane peg to the next. This was covering the 6 lanes of the track, the idea being that first past the post would have the most tape around their waist indicating the winner of the event.

It was close between first and second place. I did have most the tape around my tummy and was placed at the front of the line by the time keeper officials. We then marched to the ticket tent on the side of the track and waited for a few short minutes for our times to be recorded on the books and the tickets issued to each competitor.

A blue ticket was for first, red for second, yellow for third, green for fourth, grey for fifth and purple was for the sixth place at the finish line.

There were six competitors per race. Some events had heats due to the number of entries for that age group. My first official race event was a final and I placed first and received a blue ticket.

Later that night I lay in bed looking at my ticket. I once again felt the presence of magical spirit sitting on the bed beside me. He whispered, "How does it feel to have reached first place, to have finished in your first race as a winner?" I shared my answer quietly, "I'm actually really pleased and happy with my achievement."

"Do you think you can do that again?" he asked.

I said "Yes, it's a great feeling coming first."

Magical Spirit sat looking at my beaming smile. We spoke about the competitor that broke the gun in today's event and about my race and getting to the finish line first. Magical Spirit asked me "Can you see what I mean when I say to already see yourself winning your race on the screen of your mind?" I looked at him and said "I think I understand, I did hear you say to me today "You can do this."

"Good" said Magical Spirit. He then shared with me "I told you I would be with you to share the words of encouragement when you needed it the most. You can do this."

"Did you see this all happen on the screen of your mind today?" He asked again. I was feeling sleepy from the big day's event. I looked at magical spirit and said "I think I did. I know I saw the track with lots of people on it. I know I saw the other competitors. I did not see a clear picture of me winning yet and I don't recall any more…. Magical Spirit whispered, "We will continue in the morning for your next instalment and understanding. Rest is needed, now it's best you sleep. Then there was a silence.

Pearls of Wisdom

- ☺ I feel different, the conversations (voices) in my head was a magical feeling gearing my mind – you can do this
- ☺ My imagination (3rd eye Perception) had opened more. I could see all the people at the events. I need to get clear on my result, my own race – the gold medal I want to win.
- ☺ I felt calm and breathed through the false start. I was in my heart and in control of my actions. I knew I could win.
- ☺ The words I was saying to myself were my own words of encouragement, "you can do this". In talking to myself my intuition kept me focused.
- ☺ My body had a knowing to control the adrenaline from the false start so my muscles held me strong to go when the gun went off and not before.
- ☺ Running on the grass in bare feet was calming. The soft grass on the sole of my foot, I was connecting to my strength as Earth was grounding me. I knew I could win
- ☺ There is always an answer to the questions I ask of myself. It is best to be in a quiet space and just allow the answer to come.
- ☺ Trust my instinct that I can do something I put my mind to.
- ☺ It's ok to talk to myself and get an answer. It's good to have a conversation with myself.
- ☺ My intuition is looking out for me all the time. I just need to trust and believe it is possible.

Chapter 2

CONNECTING WITH SPIRIT

Several days later I was back on the athletics track for training. I sat on the ground remembering my first win. I also remembered the first day magical spirit spoke to me asking me to feel the experience of winning the race and can see it on the screen of my mind first. Amazing sensations of what I had imagined had come very close to be real for me.

It was now that I could see Magical Spirit in front of me again. He spoke softly "Let's pick up from where we left off from the other night as you fell asleep? Are you feeling pleased with the words I shared with you, he asked me? You can utilise this to win your first event." I sat motionless and just absorbed the words he was sharing.

He was dressed in his purple clothing, and he looked much clearer and even more vivid today. He had large open clear eyes. I could see them this time and he was sitting straight opposite me on the ground.

He asked the first question again. "Are you feeling pleased with the words I shared? You can do this to win your first event."

As I sat looking at Magical Spirit I could see he was so gentle in his manner and his voice was so soft, yet very clear. I answered "Yes", then I paused and continued, "Yes I am so pleased that I listened to your words".

"That is good" said Magical Spirit, "you could have just ignored me and proceeded on your own merit. "You may have had the same results only you would be in a different space in your thoughts". A short silence ensued as I looked towards the beautiful sparkling purple gown.

"Oh, trust me, a totally different space, said Magical Spirit. "By doing things the other way you could possibly be a bit high in the clouds, you know be a bit swollen headed, and that way does not do you any good; it could have taken you off down the wrong path". I was still sitting mesmerised by his presence and words. I was in a deep thought pondering on his words.

Magical Spirit finished his last sentence looking at me with large caring eyes. He only wanted what was best for me.

At least by listening to the voice of your magical spirit you are working with me and your own intuition and strength of knowing, you are much more confident to do it again and improve said Magical Spirit.

"Yes, that's correct", I answered.

"How did you know that I would win, Magical Sprit"? I

asked.

He sat for a moment keeping his eyes on me all the time. He took a depth breath in, "I knew by your strength, desire and determination that you wanted to do this, you wanted to win. Even if only to experience this first win and then determine that it was still right for you. I merely encouraged you with gentle words like "how fast can you do this?" So, that you could go as fast as you could to get to the finish line first". It was all about the experience for you and to know what it felt like.

"Wow" was all I could reply to Magical Spirit, "Will you be around next time I run?"

"Why, yes" said Magical Spirit, "I will be with you all the time you need me for anything you do. I'll be with you through all your endeavours and I'll guide you, I will share a way with you. It is all in the belief in yourself; to see that it is possible and then see it happen on the screen of your mind". If your imagination can dream it then you can bring it into action. You can achieve it.

I sat in awe of the purple clothed man and I just smiled. A big smile from ear to ear. I was happy with the progress, and I was learning a lot about myself at the same time. I felt confident in Magical Spirits presence and I felt strongly about winning another race. I also believed it was possible to do and that excited me.

Magical Spirit continued, "My lesson is to show you a way that you can start to see the vision of your next event occurring on the screen of your mind, and we are starting today". Everything begins with what you have as a vision for yourself.

"I am not sure when my next race is Magical Spirit", I replied.

"That's okay" he said.

"We need to start practising on getting your muscles working so that you can see anything you want to do in your life. This includes school work, your chosen career, any project you want to do, even if you want to be an entrepreneur" responded Magical Spirit. It all begins with using the muscle in your mind, this is the key to achieve.

He continued, "It takes some practice and today's a good day to start.

What we need to do is to keep your immediate focus to win your next race. So, that is what we will focus on today"[3].

What may have appeared like I was sitting on the ground daydreaming to others was Magical Spirit and myself being in a speech bubble of our own. This didn't let anyone on the outside world distract our focus and conversation. I was so focused on his soothing voice.

"So today" said Magical Spirit. "I ask you to close your eyes and sit and tell me how you felt as you won your last race.

---

[3] Note to Reader: Anything you want to achieve can also start today. Stay with a strong focus on what it is that you want to achieve. By the time, you have read this book you will have some ideas to work with for the process. Your goal, idea, plan or dream, like your dream car, your career, to be a football star, a journalist, movie star or even an entrepreneur.

What feelings did you have come up when you crossed the finish line in first place?"

What did it feel like to know you were first and you had achieved?

I sat quietly my eyes closing slowly, his voice saying "What did you feel when the other competitor broke at the beginning of the race? "Share with me what happened and how you felt" said Magical Spirit.

I sat for a moment and pondered on the question and then let the words flow out of my mouth like dancing butterflies dashing from flower to flower.

My words flowed with "It was like magic, I had this incredible feeling inside, I knew I could do this. I could achieve the blue ribbon for the first place". I went quiet; not a sound was heard. I opened my eyes to find Magical Spirit was looking back at me. I sat for a moment and closed my eyes again. I continued on "I felt the nerves and my adrenaline was racing inside of me, my heart was beating so hard I thought it would explode. I knew deep inside of me that the thought I was having was "I can do this". I only concentrated on winning and didn't put any effort or energy on how I was feeling. When the other competitor broke[4] it was like I felt a surge of confidence inside which gave me VIM. Yes, I'm going to call it VIM (Very important Magic) and it gave me the strength I could succeed with". I paused for a moment and Magical Spirit

---

[4] Broke here means left the starting position before the gun had started the race. In Athletic terms, you broke at the start

asked "What else occurred?"

I think I started to imagine a picture on the screen of my mind, I said. It was so clear to me.

Ah haa! Said Magical Spirit, "That's what I'm waiting to hear".

"What did you see and where did you see this image? He asked.

"It was kind of like a flash before my eyes. It was kind of like a magical moment of a big picture screen appeared on the inside of my forehead, and it was as if I was at the movies, yet I knew I was standing at the start of a race about to run, I said excitedly.

"That is AWESOME" said Magical Spirit, "I believe we may be getting somewhere with those comments. Could you tell me what else you saw?" he asked.

I sat quietly for a moment and pondered. I asked myself if I was I imagining all of this. Was I hallucinating? I was not really sure what was happening. Nobody had shared any information of this kind with me before so I wondered if it was normal to have this thought or vision. Was there something wrong? Was all this normal? Having not said anything to anyone before I was not sure it was normal for how my mind would operate. I wasn't even sure if it was all a part of a dream.

I hadn't spoken for a few minutes when Magical Spirit said "What did you see in those moments of thought?" I must have looked startled as Magical Spirit nodded to me "Go on".

This time I knew I had to speak, I cleared my voice and coughed gently, telling myself this is real and proceeded to answer Magical Spirit.

"For a moment when you asked the question I was right back at the start of the race. I visualised myself standing at the starting line, I saw myself getting ready to run and I heard the starter call "Take your marks".

Magical Spirit complimented "This is brilliant; you are getting it!"

"Getting what?" I responded promptly, looking rather puzzled at hearing his words.

"There is a special muscle in the brain that is known as the visualization area. It is where you can see all the things that could happen or are going to happen or have happened in your life, and once you can associate with this muscle you can turn your vision on any time to see yourself and your results," said Magical Spirit. "I can't make it happen for you all I can do is be your encouragement to see it yourself. Everyone has this muscle and some people have no idea of its strength" he said.

"What I want you to do" said Magical Spirit "is to know that this is your greatest strength. This is part of the power that is within you". "I shared earlier that whatever you can conceive you can achieve".

"What does conceive mean?" I asked. "Good question" replied Magical Spirit.

Magical Spirit took a deep breath in and shared his wisdom, "If you can see an image on the screen of your mind and it is sharing what you want to do then it is your belief and action that determines if you do it. If you can see it - you can achieve it." It all happens in the mind – just like imagination, only you can see it for you. Your intuition helps to share that it's all possible for you.

As Magical Spirit finished his last sentence he made a move to stand up. I felt as if I was in another world talking with him. Magical Spirit shared with me "We have achieved as much as possible for today. You can now understand Lesson 2. All I want you to do is to keep recalling your race until it is very clear in your mind what your next race will finish like. Where will you be in the results at the finish line?" Said Magical Spirit. 1st, 2nd, 3rd, your imagination will show you.

"I will let you think on this for a while as it is time for me to go". Magical Spirit said.

He was gone in a blink of an eye – I didn't get to say goodbye or ask when I would see him again. It all happened so quickly. I heard something happen close to me – I was drawn to this distraction.

A group of kids had arrived in the time I had been with Magical Spirit - I had no idea how much time had lapsed; it could have been hours yet I thought it was only a few minutes. It really felt like a lifetime of connection and conversation. It was such a happy place to be.

"The team coach is here" yelled one of the kids. Come on he is calling us all together so he can talk to us, come on you don't want to miss out, called one of the kids from the group.

I was standing up by this time and realising I was in my training tracksuit so I skipped over to the group of kids to listen to what the team couch had to say.

Pearls of Wisdom

- ☺ My intuition and my 3rd eye all work together, the key is to be aware.
- ☺ The voices in my head started to become stronger, guiding me and encouraging me to keep my focus strong as well.
- ☺ Speaking to myself about my race was normal as it helped me to build a stronger picture of winning the gold medal.
- ☺ Sitting quietly in a motionless position was a good thing for my body. My mind was to strengthen all the exercises I needed to do to improve my race.
- ☺ If I sit still and allow, I can see a vision with some colour of anything I want to achieve.
- ☺ I could see my strength and ability to run and I could also see myself winning any of my future races.
- ☺ My vision on the screen of my mind (inside my forehead) was real, it's a muscle I can exercise anytime I focus on the thing I want to achieve.
- ☺ I could apply this to anything in my life.

Chapter 3

TRAINING SESSIONS

As my interest grew more on achieving in this sport there was an interest in the club for the introduction of a special coach. My mum and dad looked for a coach to assist in my growth; as I was showing potential as a confident athlete. Behind the scenes, I was not aware that my new coach was to attend a training meeting on one of the local ovals. I was to realise later that bringing a special coach was an incentive by my parents in order to unlock my potentials as an athlete. The result was amazing.

As a young girl of ten years I wasn't aware of what the benefits of a coach would be and how much his assistance would help me to improve on my overall performance.

One day, during the training sessions with the coach I learnt another aspect of how powerful my mind really was. The coach had shared several new techniques with me to help improve my style of running and to assist in lengthening my stride. This was a huge challenge and one that I questioned. Why lengthen my stride? I was getting down the track as fast as I could, how would lengthening my stride have any relevance?

The coach took me aside and asked me to take a count of how many steps I took to reach the 70-meter length. I was totally unaware of how many steps it would take and proceeded to count. When this number was identified, I had to record it somewhere in my record book so as to remember the number and then to look at this in a few weeks' time after the training. This was to see if I was still taking the same number of steps or if I had learnt to stretch that little bit further and cover more distance on each step, thereby covering the distance in lesser steps, and subsequently getting to the finish line faster. It was worth it in the end. The coach's strategy really paid off!

As part of this whole process, my conversation with the coach touched a new level and I found I was reconnecting to Magical Spirit's words. What I did not know at ten years of age was that everything that occurred in day one with the connection to listen to Magical Spirit was actually going to be happening in person with my own training coach. My conversation with Magical Spirit was now going to be me in the physical form and I was about to do what Magical Spirit had shared.

How did Magical Spirit know this was going to happen?

How did Magical Spirit have any idea I would hear this information from a coach?

I was totally in awe of my coach and what he was about to share with me. I didn't know the hard yards that were ahead of me and was to learn that soon.

My coach had shared some words on what he wanted me to do, and I did as I thought I was asked to do, only to find out I had misunderstood the instruction he had given.

The coach yelled at me "when I share a technique with you see if you can visualise it happening for you", as he shuffled his large feet over the ground to where I was standing. He was not happy with my action.

I said "what do you mean?" unsure of what was going to come next. Being only ten years of age, it was a huge learning curve to know what the coach was talking about.

There were other kids on the oval with the other coaches, and having my own coach one on one made me feel pretty special. The coach was now right in front of me and looking directly at me. He didn't share this information out loud, he was very conscious to talk to me directly whilst I was standing on the track.

"When I share with you what I want you to do for each event, I want you to see yourself already doing the exercise as I have described it" said the coach. "See yourself skipping down the track".

"Do you know how to skip?" said the coach.

"Yes", I answered, and the coach said

"Can you feel what skipping is like and then see it in your mind that you are doing it yet, whilst you are standing still at the moment?"

"Wow!" I thought to myself, here is someone now talking to me about the same thing Magical Spirit has shared with me. I knew this was real as the coach was in a dark green track suit, nothing like the colours of Magical Spirit's clothing. This was happening for real. Everything Magical Spirit had shared with me was being said by my coach. Wow! how clever was Magical Spirit, I thought to myself. I was conscious of what the coach was saying.

I turned my head back to listen to the coach's word, as we had been looking down the track. He asked me to walk with him for about twenty-five yards[5,] following what he was doing. I proceeded to do as he was showing me. The little voice inside of my head said quietly to me, "All I want the body to do is run, why am I doing this hard stuff? Just let me run." I couldn't stop this internal chatter suggesting to just run; I didn't need to do this hard yard's stuff. What was going on?

It was a new thing for me to hear the internal chatter alongside the coach asking me to visualise and to be doing what I wanted to do. I was in three different places all at the same time, yet I did not know what was happening. I was about to learn.

I stopped short of the twenty-five-yard line and the coach looked back at me to see why I had stopped.

I said "this is hard; this is difficult".
"Can I just run please?"

---

[5] Old form of measure used -3 feet made one yard now known as a metre one foot was 12 inches now known as 30mm (hence the term "Hard Yards" you worked hard at it).

The coach looked at me with very stern eyes, "Yes we can just run," he went on to say "how do you think you can improve to get the gold medal?"

"Is that what you want to achieve? He asked, followed by another quick question, "Do you want to win a gold medal for the state championship events?"

I answered "Yes I did want to win".

I thought for a moment and it only seemed like a millisecond of a thought, what were the words Magical Spirit had shared back on our first contact when he asked me what winning a gold medal would feel like? What did I have to do to get the gold medal? This thought quickly flashed across my mind.

My attention and thoughts were quickly drawn back to hearing what the coach was saying "Well there is a little something that comes with training and sometimes it's called putting in some effort. I have a very special name for it."

"Yes, what's that?" I asked, thinking it was probably simple and would be easy to do.

"I call it HARD YARDS" said the coach "and hard yards means you have to put some effort into the training and you get a little something back when you do the final hard yards. The more effort you put in, the more you get back from it. Am I making some sense to you?" he asked.

I looked at him rather puzzled and thought to myself that he was asking me to make an effort and to play hard, and that way I could get a reward in having a gold medal. I proceeded to say those exact thoughts back to the coach and he answered with "Yes that is it!"

The coach went on to explain, "You can't get anywhere in life without a little effort, and those little efforts are what I call 'hard yards'. Hard yards are also known as training. Being persistent, staying on track to want to achieve. Stay with true focus to reach your goal to be a state champion athlete at a young age".

The coach looked at me and asked if his explanation was helping me to understand why it's necessary to do the hard yards. Yes, I said, I think I understand. When you are, young there is always a new way to do everything, you aim to do. However, such a young age did have its limitations. The only good thing was I did have a lot of questions, so I asked the coach as we strolled back along the track to the starting line. His advice helped me to understand more. It was to do with, "Did I believe I could do this?"

What I also felt happen was that the hard yards also aligned with the vision I saw of myself winning at other events. At the time, I didn't make a connection that what Magical Spirit shared with me was all part of the new experience I was now learning. It was to learn that what comes up as resistance is also the key element to learn to push through; these being the hard yards, which was a vital part of learning to get to the end goal.

My coach had asked me to share what my aim was at the end of the season, what did I want to achieve in my overall competition?

I sat quietly for a moment hearing all the conversation with Magical Spirit. He was asking me to share what winning a gold medal would be like.

How did Magical Spirit know I was going to have to answer this question with my coach? I shared with the coach that standing on the dais in first position to receive the gold medal was what I wanted to do. It felt good to have a gold medal around my neck for either the 70 or 100 meters. I would finish on top of the world with this result and be very proud of my achievements.

I felt a rush of happiness when I shared this with the coach and I knew what Magical Spirit had taught me and I knew I could start to see this all occurring. It was now time to share this with the coach as he was getting the feeling I had the drive and dedication to want to follow this through to the finals for a successful win.

Pearls of Wisdom

- ☺ If I can see it for myself, believe it, and stay focused, then the right people will come into my life. This is the key to building strong connections, and an application of my intuition and 3rd eye perception.
- ☺ If I focus on one thing and see it as already happening, then follow the goal to the end and stay on track all the way; doing one thing every day towards the goal, I will reach it. Whatever my heart desires, with an unwavering belief I can achieve it.
- ☺ Believing in all my chatter to myself was my encouragement that I could achieve anything I put my mind to.
- ☺ My body had to strengthen to be able to reach the distance faster, giving me the edge. I could win.
- ☺ The conversation through expression is the voice that I had within myself, to stay focused and strong.
- ☺ I had the will to want to win; all I needed to do was put it all into practice. I have the ability to see everything in my life occurring through my own visioning; all I have to do is be clear and focus on the outcome.
- ☺ Everything I see for myself is an indication of the events that will come.

Chapter 4

REFLECTION ON YOUR ABILITY

After weeks of training I had improved through my effort and doing the hard yards. I had improved a lot with my actual times for '70 meters' and '100 meters'. I was now taking longer steps down the track and my times kept improving.

What occurred for me was that I sometimes found myself on my own, especially away from the athletic track. It was on one of these occasions that I reflected on what I had been experiencing. I knew I had heard all the words from the coach speak to me and I also knew I had heard the words from Magical Spirit. What I wondered was how did this all come together.

How did Magical Spirit know I would have a coach and improve and that I really could run fast?

I sat for some time thinking what was really happening. I felt a strong feeling inside of me and I knew that I was listening to that magical voice again, only this time there was no image, I could only hear words. I wanted the image to appear and suddenly it did in a flash, only this time it was on the screen of my mind. I was seeing Magical Spirit talking to me in the vision on my screen of my mind. I felt a little puzzled as in the past I felt the image was just there, now I could both hear words speaking to me and see an image of a purple outline on the screen of my mind. Nothing was wrong, I had really connected to my higher self and was ready to act on my intuition.

I sat quietly asking myself a couple of questions, what I was to come to learn was that I was asking my higher self; my Magical Spirit, what could he see that I couldn't at that point in time. I sat on my bed in the stillness and calmness of my bedroom, and waited till I heard the voice again. It just showed me a picture of the race occurring as it happened and I just felt an extreme delight of achievement and a sense of pride as I had reached this result.

My visualisation on the screen of my mind was replaying all my events of winning each race and some of the lessons that I needed to learn. I was seeing it all occur from within the screen on my mind. It felt like I was in a moment of time inside a large bubble and all the events were happening, my eyes were closed.

I witnessed that I felt good as all this happened and I felt that I could practice this more often for all my future events. Did I need Magical Spirit anymore? Yes, I did. It was how I came to understand what was happening here. Every time I decided I was going to win an event I would sit quietly and totally keep my focus on the events that were coming. I could use the experience from the past events as a guide to improve on my next event. What I found happening may seem bizarre to the average person, however, it is what I did as a way of reassuring that what I was visualising on the screen in my head was real for me.

I attended several more training events and competed against some other experienced runners and each time this occurred I would improve, so I knew that I was doing something right. I even experienced a race where there was a staggered start and I was put to the back of the race and even though I felt it was a bit unfair I could get to the front to win. I was so determined. I can recall a picture on the vision screen in my mind as I put these words to paper. It's a strong image I used to see myself winning my events. The weeks rolled on and finally all the races of the local and regional competition events were completed and we were heading to Melbourne for the state finals.

As the family was travelling in the car to the state finals in Melbourne, I used a very clever technique to clearly see the image on the screen of my mind for the upcoming events I was competing in for the day.

As dad drove through the busy traffic towards the Athletic grounds, we had several traffic lights to cross and what I used to do was use the traffic lights as part of my race.

By this I mean dad would stop at the intersection on a red light, this was take your mark. I would line up the cars out from my window and draw an imaginary line to the next car. The yellow light was "set", and of course the green light was the gun going off. Within me the image I was using was a representation of the progress of the actual race. The stop at the traffic light was the mark, and depending on how fast dad took off, and my imaginary line to the next car, I could visualise the entire race. It was all imagination, yet I was using these tools to strengthen my focus on the result. I didn't know what this was called, or if it was normal, it just occurred very naturally for me now.

Ninety-eight percent of the time dad was very quick to get away from the start and I would win, getting to the other side of the intersection first. Sometimes I would be second, even third, depending on where the other cars were as we crossed the intersection. What occurred for me was that I was preparing my mind for my event the whole time. I was seeing myself winning all the time and this then was a confident step that I would win my event. I never drew any association to this practice until about 47 years later when I came to understand the power of the mind. What I had done as a child was focus so strongly on my end result, which was to win the gold medal.

Dad usually crossed about 40 traffic lights to reach the athletic grounds, so this was a lot of practice for seeing myself on the screen of my mind. I had already run my race and knew that I was going to win; I just didn't know how it was connected!

I'm not saying that you should use this technique of the traffic lights for your situation, all I'm saying is that it does take practice and it does mean you must have a strong focus and desire to want to achieve what it is that you see in your dream for yourself.

Anything that you believe is achievable for you is possible, the focus and determination is what is a strong connection to you succeeding.

Pearls of Wisdom

☺ My belief in Magic Spirit was real; my imagination showed me ways of bringing it all together, with the first step being to believe in myself.

☺ My heart knew it felt good so I kept doing it – a knowing that it was all helping. It felt good each time dad made it across the intersection first, and this gave me a real sense that I had won the race.

☺ My intuition guided me all the time, at such a young age I just followed as it happened. It felt good and I felt in alignment, I would sit still and let the thoughts flow.

☺ 3rd eye perception became so strong that Magic Spirit didn't need to be in the image form all the time, I could hear him speaking to me from the inside. I came to know he was with me.

☺ My expression through my voice led me to have small conversations with myself. I knew I could do this again. I had achieved it once and I could do it again. Positive talk to me was that I will achieve.

☺ Any time I stood on the athletic track I felt grounded, it was like a magnetic strip for me. I always felt alive and vibrating on the track. I did not want to be still. I felt a sense of feeling so connected to earth it boosted my power of connection.

☺ My body was strong and in good strength. I had trained several times and I was eating good meals to assist in strength. I could feel the sensation of

- muscles in my body during different times when I visualised myself on the track.
- If I keep my focus strong on the screen of my mind and practice using it every day anything can happen with a positive result.
- Believing and doing the training (hard yards) are all part of the end results and were vital ingredients in the success of the achievement.
- The words I hear for myself are an indicator of the action to take.
- The vision I see is my highest focus to aim for.

Chapter 5

VISUALISATION TO REALITY

Whenever I needed to really focus I would often feel Magic Spirit around me, guiding me and helping me with my preparation in training and the competition events on the days they occurred. I had come to really use my visualising for many aspects of my athletic races. At ten years of age, in my first competition at the state championships I was to learn so much about who else could also run fast. I did not really understand the depth of competition for an event at this time. All I recall is that I had to run and run fast was what I did. I knew that I would have to go through several races and wins to progress to the next event. I was fortunate to win most of the time with a few seconds here and there.

I used to sit quietly until my race time and in this time, I would see my race occurring and where I finished for each practice I did. This was all that I focused on. I had myself winning the race every time before the race was run. I used to use the time in the preceding events at the starting line to visualise it was me on the starting blocks getting a great start before my race was even called.

The state event was the culmination of all the competitions in the local team competition for the district events, then the regional championship; and now here I was at the Victorian State Championship events. Competitors were all around and I had not run against them before, and thus I had no idea of what they could achieve. I did not know any of them and what their achievements were. It was interesting times just talking amongst ourselves and comparing personal event times etc. I used to use this to my advantage as I never gave out the correct race times for an event, especially when I could run faster than the time I was told. I learnt early not to give too much away. One day, one girl said to me "you hadn't run as fast as I and yet you beat me". I can't recall what I said, I just learnt it was best not to share my fastest times too openly and to play down how fast I had run and trained. I felt it gave me an edge. It kept the competitors guessing, yet for me I knew I would be faster. I already had faster times.

I had also learnt as part of my training that it was not about what they could do, it was about what I could do. It was about the race I was about to win not about if they could beat me or if I could beat them. As my coach taught me, irrespective of their position in the race, my aim was to be the winner; crossing the finish line first, and that was all I could focus on.

My practice of being able to see the race in my mind was a huge indicator to me that I was going to succeed. I had trained, done the hard yards and I had visualised so many times to see myself already winning.

I could see myself on the dais with the gold medal around my neck. I could hear Magical Spirit asking me what it felt like and I shared with him. I felt extremely happy and excited. Proud of all my efforts. A really good feeling that glowed from the inside. Spirit was with me all the time, he shared a spot in my mind and every time I felt I needed to focus Spirit would have a conversation with me. I trusted this occurring and went on to win. I just had a good feeling inside of me that I could call on my power strength as I had done the hard yards of training and I knew inside that I could win gold.

- § -

I sit here today with visions of those days flooding back to me. I can see a short girl from Geelong who I had heard was going to be strong competition and truly she was. I knew very little about her ability as we competed separately in our heats for the 70-meter event. I think from memory I had a semi-final and then I competed beside her in the final event for this short distance.

Everyone had run their race and was being given a ticket indicating what their time was for the event. It was only in some cases that the first two place getters moved through to the finals or only the first place that reached the finals. I must have finished first for each event as here I was in the final of the seventy meters and I was also a finalist for the 100 meters' sprint. The young runner from Geelong was in the final as well. This was going to be a good race. My focus was only on the event, not the other competitors, and my goal of standing in first place on the dais at the end of it all. All I could see was the finish line. Spirit had crossed my path again, only this time it was in words of encouragement, "You can do this, you're strong and tall. Remember all those steps, you learnt to take a longer step in training, here is the time you need to put this all into action and get to the finish line first". I did this several times on the

A VISION TO WIN

screen of my mind. I heard Spirit whisper in my ear, I felt his presence in my body, I knew I would win, I could win... I visualised myself winning my race. I could see Hayley[6], my competitor was a little bit nervous and I guess I was too, I just didn't show it as much.

Haley was from Geelong Victoria and she was champion for her region, while I was from the South Gippsland region. We had both competed in our local events and entered the regionals and succeeded in those events, leading us to be in the state final championships. It was quite a feat for each young girl to achieve, and we were both keen to win again. There were several children from both regions and from the rest of the state all competing for the State Championship.

(Refer page 72 Pearls of Wisdom)

---

[6] Haley is the name used for the purpose of this book it is not the real name of the actual person. No permission was given to use the physical personal name; so, Haley is a story name only

Chapter 6

PEOPLE PROJECT THEIR THOUGHTS AND FEELINGS ALL AROUND YOU

Now I will digress for a moment and share with you a story of what was happening to my mum as she sat in the grand stand. Mum was minding her own business, looking and watching closely at the upcoming event that I was about to compete in when she overheard two ladies making comments about the girls standing at the starting line. Much of the comment was about me as I stood so tall and was more developed than the other girls. Much was said about my height, that I must have been in the wrong age group and that there would have to be a protest against me if I should win the event. Little did the women talking know that mum was sitting in front of them in the grandstand. I'm unable to recall if the race was run or not at this point in time, however, mum turned around and said "that's my daughter you are referring to and no she is not in the wrong age group. She is in the right age group and in fact also won all her regional events up till this point.

To be in the age group I was in I had to meet some criteria that gave me a small edge. The ages started at Under 9's, Under 10's Under 11 and Under 12's registration. Your birthday was taken as at the 1st October of the year and that indicated what age group you competed under. I was 9 years old on the 1st of October so I run under 10's. My birthday was 2nd October so this gave me a small edge to be the age I was running under and still be in my same age group. I was tall for my age and a very solid build.

One can only imagine what the women did when my mum made that comment to them. It was not that they could move to another part of the grandstand and find a new seat as it was already at full capacity. Mum and the ladies were sitting at the end of the race to see the finish as best as they could.

Mum had her own focusing to do, she was to watch her daughter perform at a top level for her age in her first competition at the state level championships. A lot of time and effort on my parents' part had been shared for me to be at this top level. The best I could do was to win.

For whatever the other parent was projecting, the fact that Haley was there indicated she was a good runner; she had probably faced as much competition as me or maybe it been easy for her to win everything, neither of us were to know. It was the first time we had met in competition. This race was going to be the key indicator of who was the quickest and better sports person to win the gold.

There is silence in the crowd as the Marshalls call the competitors to stand in front of their lanes. It was time. The race was about to begin and a silent hush murmurs over the grandstand.

(Refer page 72 for Peals of Wisdom)

Chapter 7

TALL POPPY

The starter said "Take your mark…., Set." And the gun goes off.
I take a flying leap from the starting blocks to have a good start in front of the race. As I am running down the straight the Geelong gal is there, however, I gain speed and inch by inch move closer to the line to win the event. My first achievement in state championships. It was also about this time that I came to understand that having confidence to win was not enough to win a race. Hayley from Geelong had not lost a race and was so confident that she was going to win. She may have won her heat and regional events to be at the state championships, however, she had not anticipated for another competitor to come out and beat her. In the finals, it was I who beat her and another lass. I remember the memory fondly as I look at the photo of us on the dais.

Hayley came 3rd place in the finals. Sometimes it can be a hard lesson to learn about defeat when we feel so confident to win. As for me it was a great lesson to learn.

Spirit had told me that sometimes to lose is your greatest challenge, to get up and win again was no easy feat. It does something to you if you are strong, focused and determined. I know at one of my final events I ran an easy second as I wanted to reserve energy for the finals. I only had to run in the first to get to the finals. Whilst this may have been a game plan to create, it's not always a good tactic. Sometimes you have to go hard to get to the front of the race and in doing so you can spend all your energy. Hayley had been a huge success for her region and she had won all her division's competitions. Nevertheless, getting to the finals was not as 'cruise' as she may have first thought. Never take your eye off the finish line. The focus is always on the finish line so make sure you finish where you want to be. And if others are faster than you and finish ahead of you, be thankful for the experience. It will be the best experience you could have so that you are hungry for your next run.

In writing this book I have been sent on a walk down memory lane only to find all my tickets and medals of events. My medals sit close to my heart in a padded bag in my bedroom. They have faded a wee bit and worn from the shiny colour there were on the day. Magnificent and all as they are, it brings a tear to my eye how proud I am of my achievements and in saying this I inspire you, the reader, to really take the tips I'm sharing and the concepts written in this book to achieve your dreams and goals in life.

Is it going to be hard yards?

Yes, it is.

Is it going to be an easy road to the top?

No, it's not.

Your ability to keep your focus in line with where you want to be and look to the result. You must know what to visualise on so that it is in line with your result. This also includes sitting quietly and meditating on the goal at hand to see to its achievement. You must be determined to do the hard yards and practice for the outcomes you wish to achieve.

So, no matter who your competition is, you must get out there and win your race. It may not only be a race in sport, it may be in everything in life, there is always going to be other competition. Everything in life is about the element of competition, and I don't mean that in a negative competitive way. I mean it's a lesson in life to realise that you can do anything you put your mind to. It's a prompt that whatever that dream is within you, is there for you, and you can achieve it, you just must believe it's possible for it to be achieved.

Keep your focus. Be clear on your goal – make a written description of the result you want to achieve and most of all, be true to yourself. Give yourself a date to achieve your goal by setting steps you want to achieve along the way. The written goal helps to materialise your goal with some haste.

Follow your intuition and stay focused - Stay focused and STAY FOCUSED.

Your visualisation of your dream will keep you on the right path towards your goal.

Chapter 5; 6; 7; - lessons gained

Pearls of wisdom

☺ Magical spirit is always there, it's your perception or what thoughts you are having that is the outcome of your events.
☺ Heart feels good and you feel positive about the results you are having and you feel in flow to achieve. Everything feels like it's in alignment to your end goal.
☺ Intuition keeps you in alignment if you listen to your inner voice. Intuition and 3rd eye perception all speak together with what you want to do and it all feels good.
☺ When everything is in alignment your body will feel good, no hesitation or tension, you will be in flow.

Chapter 8

POSITIVE SELF-TALK – TOUGH COMPETITORS

When I first started in competition races, it was always hard to know who was fast and who you could beat, it was kind of like a game of run and catch them if you can. It wasn't until I started with my actual training days that I really came to understand how positive my attitude was and how my thoughts would be a good indicator of my end results.

Back on the athletic track for another season and I felt Spirit around me again, I was a year older and so some of the dedication had waned and the focus had to be brought back into alignment for this next season. As the season, had just started and the previous year I had learnt a lot, it was not until the real competition started that my coach came back onto the scene. We had the team coach for the local athletic group that meets every Saturday and we did the extra training through the week as the competition heated up. Most of my competition was good, I would sometimes be beaten in a race and if I won easily I was put up to the next age group competition to run hard against. This was good incentive as it had me run faster to be in the top three. My own age group was good as well and I had two other girls who were always close to me in the first 3 place getters. However, they did not always win. It really depended on the event we were racing against. Longer distance they could pass me to the finish line first.

In my younger school days, my running events would be 50 yards' sprint in the school yard running in the lanes all marked out with bailing twine[7], it was a kind of string that was strung between sticks in straight lines forming lanes.

Most of the time it was at the sound of a whistle or someone singing out "GO" and then be called a cheat because you might have run before they said the word "go". I must have been around 8-9 years of age when I first competed in a running event as we knew them in those days.

Athletics was to be a word I would learn when I was closer to 10. There were two girls at primary school that I would run very close to. Most of the times it was a dead heat for every running event. There was not a lot that could separate us 3 at these short distance events. The three of us all competed against one other, while we played in the local district netball team together and won our first netball grand finale. That was a close match in the grand final for a young team. The Korumburra Dolphins Netball team and the Kongwak Junior team in the grand final and then the final score being 16-12 in our favour. Learning how others cope with defeat was a great lesson to learn at a young age. We learn so much from our parents' habits. I was grateful to learn the art of defeat and the ability to win with pride.

---

[7] Bailing twine – it was a light weight string of many threads that was used to hold bales of Hay together at harvesting time. It was an endless piece of string that could unravel for a long way.

Whenever I was on the track for an event, I had a knowing inside of me that I would do well. The school athletic events at the local district competition were only a short trip down the road to the recreation oval where the running track was laid out. The events were quite different from the athletic events nowadays. We had a lot of opportunity to have fun with different events. The district's region of schools would all gather in their coloured bibs so that you knew which school was what and who was competing on the day.

The coloured flag representing the school stood at each bay where all children had to assemble. Some of the events we competed in were the sack race, the egg and spoon race and the skipping race. There was a lot of competition and lots of events to watch including high jump, long jump, and triple jump.

Some of these events at the School Regional Championships also had my name as a record holder, especially triple jump and long jump. However, both my younger sisters did improve on my distances. My youngest sister still holds the record today at the local Primary School in Victoria we attended for the triple jump. My jump in 1968 at 11 years of age was 26ft 5 ¾ inches (7 meters 900 centimetres), then in 1969 at 12 years of age I hopped, stepped and jumped (triple jump as it is known today) 29ft 11½ inches. (9 meters and 30 centimetres 9.30). Later in the same year I triple jumped 33 feet (10meters 58 centimetres 10.58) in an athletic competition at the State Championships which won me a bronze medal for placing in 3rd position.

As far as I am aware, my younger sister still holds the record today with a triple jump of approximately 32 feet (9.754 meters). It has been a record now at Kongwak State School, Victoria for 41yrs.

My sisters were also good athletes in their day to be able to still hold records for these events.

- § -

As much as Spirit kept me in alignment with my end goals, I was always talking to myself quietly inside, giving myself the confidence to succeed in these events, regardless of the competition I was against. It was hard to stay focused when you knew it was something you wanted to do well at, and it was hard to do as well, every little bit of training helped during these tougher races.

There came a time when I was unsure what I would do and which distance or events I was to run. I also liked to compete in the walking events and it wasn't until one day when I shared the news with my coach that I was to find out I was using different muscles for a walking event compared to a sprinting event. He was very clear that to win a gold medal I had to make a choice between walking events or sprinting events. I chose sprinting.

What distance would I run? What training would I prepare for? What was my highest love in athletics? What did I enjoy the most? Where did I see was the best for me?

I had run the '100meters' and really enjoyed the speed of that event. The '200 meters' also had a rush to it as well. I did not favour the '400 meters' though many said I ran a good race when I did run. I loved the long jump as well, and the triple jump, so these were the areas I concentrated on.

Once I had my focus I was not allowed to ride my bicycle at home, especially when the state championships were on, as my coach told me I was using completely different muscles and this may affect the overall performance so that was a treat I had to forgo until the event was over.

Was it hard? Of course, my sisters whizzed past me on their bikes while I had to walk or jog everywhere I went.

At the time, I thought it harder and a punishment, however, I was to be rewarded with a gold medal for all my efforts. At the young age of ten in the Victorian Little Athletics Association I was to achieve a huge milestone of being on the dais with medals around my neck for two events. At age ten I ran second in the '70 meters' and first in the '100 meters'.

So, for me it was about what race I would run, and when I concentrated on the 100 and 200 I was really feeling in my element. As the years progressed and I developed into a sprinter, so did the competition around me. I again achieved 1st in the 70 meters and second in the 100 at 11 years of age, and in my 12th year I was successful in the 100, coming 3rd place, and finishing 3rd in the triple jump. Despite running in the 200 meters' race in the regional championship I was never successful to reach the state finals for this event. The competition had improved.

In my twelfth year, there were a few changes as the body changed with puberty and I carried a bit more weight, I still could move fast despite my size, however, it was a lass from Mildura that won the '100 meters' sprint and a competitor that I used to compete against to get into the finals at the regional events that also won against me in second place. I finished third.

I also had the opportunity to run in the Victorian School Girls Championships which was a very exciting day for me. In the days leading up to the event, I was to read in the state newspaper of the upcoming event with a possible champion in the making. A young girl from Mildura whom the reporters thought was a real high-success athlete. Her picture and her times were recorded in the newspaper.

Dad called me to the kitchen table and said "what's your fastest time for '70 meters', I want to compare it to this report in the paper" My times were faster than what was printed in the newspaper and the school Girls' Championships was only days away. The competition day arrived and I had competed in my 1st heat. It was in this race I believe I beat this lass only to have her win the finals and I finished second. It was an excellent effort for a twelve-year-old school girl's championship. This young girl from Mildura was then successful in the Victorian Little Athletics Championships as she won the 100 metres sprint in a speed of 12.8, second was 12.9 and I finished third with a time of 13.2.

1970 was a good year, lots of achievements and lots of success. As life moved forward I was to become aware there was to be an Australian Little Athletics Competition that was held at night at the Victorian Olympic Athletic Park. I missed out on being selected in the overall Victorian team, however, I was to be invited to run in a special invitation race at this event under the lights. What an experience and credit to me. I was 12 when this event occurred.

It was not my most favourite event as I had not concentrated to run the 400 meters and this was the event I was asked to compete in by invitation. What an honour to be considered to participate in this event. I then approached my coach to identify how to run 400 meters, as there was an art to be able to reserve strength so that the final 100 you still had a sprint inside. I was to have a couple of nights' crash training only running 400's. Thank goodness I was still fit from the recent championships. The event was to be a night event at Olympic Park Melbourne.

A VISION TO WIN

The starter called us to take your marks. I'm not sure what lane I was in, however, I think it was about the middle of the field, which I was happy with. I can recall it was a very close event. I ran 1minute and 04 seconds, finishing 4th just outside the medals. 1st ran 1:2.5 seconds, while 2nd ran 1:3.0 seconds and 3rd was 1.03.7 minute. So, in looking at the speeds you can see it was a very close finish to a very special event. To be fourth best in Australia at the age of 12 was a huge achievement. I still feel very proud of this moment today. 1.5 seconds between 1st and 4th.

Now here is something for you to consider. I have looked at my memorabilia and can find that the actual times for the Victorian State Championship competition for the Under 12 Girls were a close event as well.

1st place ran 1:2:7, 2nd place was 1:4:5 and 3rd was 1:4:7. It looks like the invitation event run was faster than the actual state final. I have a copy of the finals events that I draw that reference from. Quite an achievement I'd say. It was very special especially when all the competitors of this '400 metres'-event missed out on being selected for the respective Australian competition on the night. This was a special event on the night of the Australian Little Athletic Event, which was held by invite only.

- § -

Being in the starter's hand was a nervous time, however, getting a flying start was another question. Being disqualified was so hard. Let's move on to hear the starter say …

"Take your Marks" - "Se…..t"…

Pearls of Wisdom

☺ Being in connection to your highest self and listening to the inner voice does have impact on the results you achieve.
☺ What you think about comes about. Keep your thoughts on the positive outcome in all aspects of your life.
☺ Negative chatter in the form of doubt, fear and procrastination, unsure moves and no focus, walking aimlessly is all controlled by you. Being aware of the chatter is a huge key to taking steps to listen to yourself and move forward with lots of little steps towards the end goal.
☺ When your heart is connected to the end goal, nothing will get in your way. Being aware of this focus is the real success in anything in life.

Chapter 9

PERFECTING YOUR TECHNIQUE - FLYING STARTS; HOW TO SEE IT ALREADY ACHIEVED

I was sitting on the ground at the start of the 100 meters watching all the kids start their races before me. I was again in the presence of Magical Spirit; it was like we moved to another field not seeing or hearing anyone around us…we were in a world of our own. It was like the speech bubble I mentioned earlier, I was totally in a daze with him.

Magical Spirit shared, "It's getting close to the finals again, how do you think you can set yourself to be a winner once more?" I sat for a few short seconds looking at him; this wise man was wearing his beautiful purple gown which shimmered in the sunlight. He was looking at me with so much encouragement and guidance.

"Improving on my starting techniques, coupled with learning how to use my feet in the right way and get the push off when the gun goes off would be a big help. Being able to have a flying start would also be a great help", I shared back with Magical Spirit, "Or even learn how to use blocks[8] to really have something to push off from at the start."

"Well," said Magical Spirit, "this is a great start to boost you off the blocks as they are called. Lets' see what we can do to have this all happen, then you'll be able to see the improvement for you". Magical Spirit kept sharing with me all the time and I knew I was doing everything right. He kept the encouragement up and told me whenever I had shown improvements in my events. I always heard a whisper of congratulation from afar. I knew it was my Magical Spirit sharing with me. Magical Spirit shared with me that having starting blocks[8] would help, however, it would only be for practice sessions as they were not allowed in the junior competition. A set of blocks were coming, I just needed to be patient. He moved out of my image again. My race was close to being called. I was ready to step up to the starting line and win another event. Focus was needed here and I concentrated to be ready, I was listening for my name to be called.

As I improved and gained more and more technique, I then advanced to using spikes[9] for my sprinting, this assisted in the starts as I had slipped at the starting line a few times in the past. My coach also saw my potential and introduced me to a new technique he called the crouch[10] start, this had me improve in my sprint times and overall technique. It was such a new way to look at a race. I could kneel in the starting position, look at my race from this lower perspective and work out where I would be gaining

---

[8] Blocks were an instrument used to assist you on the starting line for your feet so you had a good start and did not slip
[9] Spikes are Shoes with a metal nail like out of the base of the shoe, children's spikes have a knob on the base of the shoe this helps to hold grip on the ground and not slide
[10] Crouch start is a position where you crouch down on the ground to get a good push off from the ground (refer pic on page 89)

full speed after rising from this crouch start immediately the gun went off.

Gazing down the track, visualising myself running whilst focusing on crossing the line in first place were all images in my mind. These images were all in order and I was quietly talking to myself about the race as well.

It was fun times getting this all into practice and realising the potential to improve on my overall times over each distance. Learning how to run from this new position took some practice. I was used to standing starts as I was already training hard for the overall events so to add a start technique into the practice was not too hard. It all assisted in getting a perfect start. A flying perfect start.

So, what is a flying start?

It's a start that involves a standing start at the start of the race and a reacting quickly off the mark. However, as much as these starts have some benefits for running there is always a possibility of slipping from your feet on the ground surface. The flying start was to anticipate the starter's gun going off at the precise time. In fact, you leave the blocks/start as the gun smoke is seen, the gun going off is the noise you react to for you to run. Going too soon was classed as a false start, going as the gun went off was a flying start.

Let's go back to the way in which we visualise, being told that one needs to be aware of the crouch start and how to control your muscles so that you lean forward with the right amount of pressure, yet having all the power in your legs to push you from the blocks. Learning this position took some practice to achieve what the right position to hold was. Watching others compete from this position seemed to give them a small edge; they were off to a flying start totally from the beginning of the race, giving them a small advantage right from the start. The key was having the speed to end the race with full stamina and not lose any momentum during the race. Being able to use your muscles and visualise seeing yourself holding your position in place at the start took a lot of practice.

It took lots of experimenting to get the position right before I really gained the full effect of using this crouch position for my events. Once I perfected it I used it all the time. The next added bonus was using the starting blocks pushed into the ground so that they gave you a solid push off point.

Now to add to this I had to hold my body in a perfect position that was not leaning too far forward (or I would lose balance and fall), this lean forward had to be precise so that there was enough power for push off in my legs. The momentum gained from the push off had your arms swing in a way that lifted you from the start to lean forward and gain more momentum.

Now using your muscles to control your balance and your mind to stay focused on the first 5-10 steps was a critical point of getting out of the blocks with an advantage. Secondly, being able to anticipate the gun going off so that you really got a great start was the next factor of a flying start. It was all in the critical timing of the count of the starter. "Take your marks", now when all are settled the word "Set" is next and then on the count of 2-3 seconds the gun would go off - BANG! Learning to be so comfortable with the timing was an edge, if you held too long you would not go on the gun, if you went too soon it was a false start. It all took huge amount of practice.

Take your marks ...two...three   SET! Two...three Bang!!! You're off running down the track.

I could master this several times, once or twice a false start

was called as I left the blocks just a whisker before the gun went off and had to really control my mind and muscles for the second restart of the race. What was worse was if this (false start) then occurred a second time and it was not you that broke, then you really had to be with a strong focus to wait for the gun on the next start. Practising that was a huge impact; learning how to be so controlled over the nerves and keenness to want to run was a difficult task. I remember doing a drill on this for possibly an hour or so; it seemed that long at the time, I know I learned a lot at that time and my start became more proficient.
Afterwards I had little to no breaks and flying starts all the time.

I will endeavour to share this as much as I can to give you a sense that you are on the blocks at the start of your race, say 100 meters, the competition is strong and you want to get to the end first. Your body may feel some nervous tension; this only adds to the adrenaline. A lot of times it felt like butterflies in your stomach or sometimes an empty feeling, or you could be sick. Those never happened; I only had a feeling inside of nerves inside of me.

The starter calls the competitors to the starting line. You hear the words "TAKE YOUR MARKS". There is a tingle in your body, you want to jump, yet you need to be so focused on the race ahead of you. You have a spring in your step. You lower the body into a crouched position so that you rest on your hands close to the starting line. Raising your more powerful leg into in the blocks first, you then lower yourself to your knees. Your stomach starts to settle and you are able to take a deep breath, ready to push off from the blocks.

You're constantly feeling the muscles in your legs pumping so that you have all the reserved energy to push off when the gun goes off. You are looking towards the ground to find the line and keeping your body straight and in alignment with your feet so that when the gun goes off you are in a straight line for projection. You have lifted your head to look no more than 10 meters in front of you so that you can gauge where you need to be; well and truly upright and into full momentum as you fly from the blocks. In this position, you can feel most relaxed and ready, your shoulders will flex and only when you feel your muscles in the right position will your head look to the ground. Only when I am totally still does the starter know I'm ready. You await the words 'SET' from the starter's voice.

When you can see in your mind's eye that you have passed that 10-meter mark from the start and you are in full upright can you then look further down the track to run the race in your mind to the finish line. By 20 meters you are well into form and gaining speed. It's a process and an accurate one at that to make sure everything is in perfect position for your race.

I was still running my race in my mind's eye before the race even started.

I share all of this as a way of showing what depth I had in focus, being able to visualise what I was going to do. I visualised myself in this position, felt my muscles at the right lean and hold for 2-3 seconds waiting for the gun to go off. These are all facets of visualising. I was constantly doing this so that I could execute it perfectly in all my races. In some cases, it was a natural process, while on other days I can say I knew when I had not performed well. I could tell whenever I had not used my visualisation technique with strong focus as an added advantage for that race. It applies to all facets of our life as well.

Talk about controlling your muscles on the starting blocks, listening to your heart beat, feeling the urge to push off the blocks strong. I had to visualise this occurring before the race was run, I had to feel and know where that angle of my start was so that I did not fall. I had to know in my mind that to get it right I had to practise it all the time in my focus. I had to be with a steady control so that it sunk into my mind strength and was impregnated every time I visualised a crouch start.

That is what visualising is all about, seeing yourself already in the mind's eye achieving the result you are aiming for, being able to sense the feeling of your muscles in the correct position, knowing it was the best outcome towards your achievements.

It's all about muscle control, it's about focus, and it's about visualising all aspects for everything we do. Only when we have it implanted in our brain so significantly can we do it confidently and work towards our end goal.

- § -

Let's look at a gymnast; either male or female, both have a set routine to do for their performance on the parallel bars. How do you think they can do it so perfectly and gain a ten at any Olympic event if they have not visualised the routine in their head?
Practise is part of the process, and so is visualising; using muscle memory, knowing how much effort that is needed to make it to the next element of the routine. Gymnasts sit and visualise their routine regularly. It's in their mind and they use their muscles to know what strength is needed for the execution of each part of the routine. The other element is also a very deep feeling that one can feel inside that they know it's right for them to do. This feeling can be referred to as a Spiritual connection of faith that it will all work out. It only takes a split second to lose one part of the focus and you can be on the ground so fast if the mind is not totally routed with the precise information

of the exercise.

Let's also consider a singer – They must know the lyrics of the songs they sing. They are in tune with the music; it resonates and vibrates with them. They can visualise the words at any point of music played. This is being with a conscious competence that allows them to be in tune with the music and lyrics every time they sing. The lyrics are set in the memory bank of the mind, they visualise the music and sing the words as they perform.

Sometimes doubt may creep in and this takes the focus off your achievements, or in the case of a singer they forget the lyrics, while the gymnast doesn't remember the routine and falls…it's all part of the process to stay with a clear vision of succeeding. It's also the hard yards of the training that brings you to the success of the event you are doing.

- § -

On one particular day at practice after I was introduced to using starting blocks, I put the blocks in the ground back to front and nearly came close to falling at the start. This was a huge learning curve for me. I didn't do that again. It was a huge realisation that I needed to really be focusing on the placement of the blocks for all my starts.

The main thing of any starting crouch position was to be able to hold your set position for a period of approximately 2-3 seconds before the gun went off. It was in this set position that some starters held for a longer period and some just right. If you broke in this time, then you were issued with a warning. You were only allowed two breaks and then it was disqualification from that event.

It only happened to me once that I can recall and I may

have broken as a way of getting off the mark quickly, however, I never experienced being disqualified at a major event.

Having a flying start was such a great advantage. It happened often for me and when it did it always led to good results.

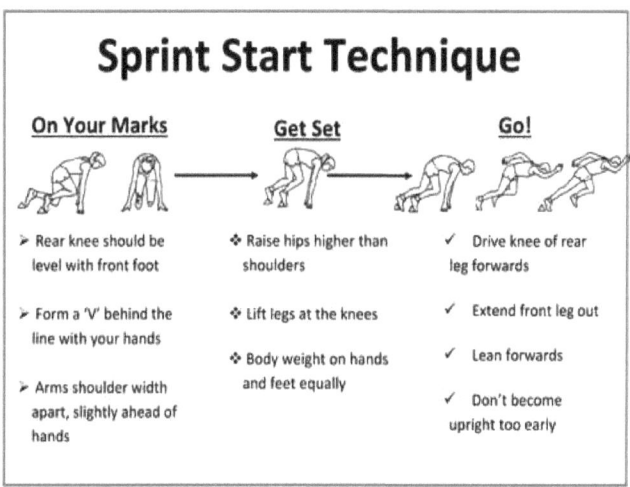

For me, getting a good start was an indication of winning the race or coming second. I loved the feeling of being in front of the race and loved the times when I had to work a bit harder to catch them. It's all a matter of what you believe is possible and all can be achieved where ever you are in the race, not just in an athletic race.

When the Starter calls you to take your marks you are still allowed to take a little extra time to get settled into the crouch start position. It was not an immediate position you could get into. I would visualise my start as getting off the mark quickly and to be in front. I would partition the 100 meters into 4 parts. This is how I saw the race as I sat at the start, getting into the crouch position.

First 25 meters - use this momentum to get away fast, building up my speed and stride, and gaining momentum. 25-50 meters - really start to pick up pace, while keeping my eye on the finish line all the time. 50-75 meters - really stretch out the stride so that I have a wee bit in reserve and then plant my foot to increase speed at the 75-meter mark, ready for the last 25 metres to the finish. There were some days when I ran another 25-50 meters through the finish line I was going so fast. Those days were good and I knew I was at top speed. There was nothing worse than coming to a sharp stop at the end of the race after being at top speed. That's how an injury can occur.

The feeling you get when you make that transition from high speed to a gradual stop after crossing the finish line is exhilarating, especially when you know you are in the top 3 finishers. All of this was going on before I had even run my race…it all happened in a very short space of time. I run my race in my mind's screen before I have even completed the race. Remember the traffic intersection; I had run my race in my head before the race was run. This is a huge awareness to have for all sporting events, even when you have a goal that you want to achieve in everyday life.

Can you see yourself winning your race, whatever that may be? Life is a form of a race all the time; we have lots of little challenges happening all the time. Nothing is different for sport or for anything you want to achieve in life.

You may wish to plan for a big trip or audition for a singing contest, or even go for a job in the field of your choice. Your thoughts are in indicator of your end results. Your feelings and how you perform on the day also have impact on the result.

Are they negative thoughts or positive thoughts?

Will you be a success or not?

Life shares so many chances with you and for you, it's being aware of all the chances that come your way that is key.

Let us go a step further. Consider to read first then….

Close your eyes, think of what it is you want to achieve in your life, whatever that is. Can you visualise this on the screen of your mind?

Can you see yourself achieving this? (Whatever 'this' is for you)

Can you sit quietly to think and imagine what it is that you would like to achieve?

There is nothing wrong if you can't, sometimes it may be in a feeling you have and you know you will do everything possible to reach this outcome. Everyone has a screen in their mind, some only use it half the time so it's not well practiced and others have to dig a wee bit deeper to see their vision. Or if you are like me you can see it instantly without any practice – this feels good. Everybody is right where they are with this technique, nobody is wrong it's just where you are in this moment. It's in your awareness, some people may need to learn more about this process to be able to use it fully.

When I was in some races I would find myself in midfield and this was challenging for me. Somewhere inside of me I would find something, I have no idea what I could even call it, I just knew I could find some extra speed. I would shift my body into a new gear if that is the right way to describe it. I would lengthen my stride and start to really find extra energy to move through the competitors and move to be in the top three. Now a lot of things are happening in this short space of time. I am running, I am aware of where I am in the field, and I'm also working out a strategy on how to shift from my place in the field to the top three. 13 seconds is not very long when you have all of this to think about, yet I did do this to achieve 1st, 2nd, or 3rd position in a race.

I can recall a feeling of being in a race and shifting a gear. I can also recall a race where I completely collapsed from engaging this ability only to find myself on the ground at the end exhausted from lack of training.

What I find amazing now is that I have not exercised for some years to the same level with any real intensity and I have this urge in me to want to do better whenever I had a personal trainer (PT). The PT could see me improving week by week, something at the cellular level just kicks in to do better with any sporting effort I aim to do.

I had recently stepped back onto the athletic field and I felt such a connection with this when I trained a young girl. She wanted to be a state champion in the events she had entered. It's an awesome feeling to have such a connection and such a drive to want to help her. It feels so good when you are doing something that really is in tune with what you are doing. You may just find that it's a wee bit easy to do. Now it's not easy in the sense that you don't have to train and still just go and do it, what I am saying here is that you feel in complete connection with the event or thing you are doing and it feels good to do. This is an indication of you being in flow, being able to achieve anything you set your mind to. Sometimes you will just have a knowing that whatever it is you are doing is right, because if it's hard to do and you are not enjoying it then maybe it's not the right thing (*) to be doing.
(*Define "thing"- any event, effort, action, purpose, job, or training that you are doing at any given time).

Can you see how the connection from the flying start was always something I excelled at and this had me in a good place for the overall race, whereas if I missed the start and got away on the gun I had to work a wee bit harder. I had to push the hard yards to get momentum into action. This being so much harder, I could still do it, However, it only led to a much closer finish at the finish line.

Pearls of Wisdom

☺ Magic Spirit refers to your inner knowing of what you know you are doing. When it feels good and you feel like you are in flow then you are more likely to do well. The feeling of knowing is unique for us all; we all have a special thing in life we all do well. Staying in tune with this is a key and an indicator of our true path to follow.

☺ Heart alignment with this flow often has things happen a wee bit faster when you are having this feeling. It feels good so we do more. Heart keeps us true to our self and we just are aligned to all the good if we avoid the outside chatter.

☺ Intuition is when we have a vision of the result play in our mind and we already see ourselves achieving the result. Intuition gives us many signs and sometimes we ignore them all and go another path only to come back and say I should have done this in the first place. We are often offered training in a specialist field or someone offers us an opportunity and we knock it back that is intuition talking to us on many levels. Sometimes we just are not aware of the importance of the message or opportunity.

☺ Third eye perception already sees the event unfold. The race was in front of me yet the 3rd eye played in my mind over and over as I ran the race. It's another indicator of the path to follow.

☺ Expression of Voice connects us with the depth of what we want or do not want as the words we speak are the indicator. Being mindful that I didn't want to do something the coach was sharing; did I really want to win the race was the coach's question back to me. My voice had a say, however, it was an objection and it needed to be silenced or fear or doubt could have crept in.

☺ Body is the vehicle in which we get around. Body is also the muscle structure that helps us to reach for that goal, whether we need to stretch harder or just push ourselves to reach some certain criteria. I had to learn to know what muscle strength was to hold in the starting position. Today that cellular level of muscle still knows what to do…it is ingrained in us.

Chapter 10

BEING PART OF A TEAM RELAY RACES... YOU CAN'T VISUALISE FOR ANYONE ELSE - ONLY FOR SELF

I was lying on my bed one day and daydreaming of my athletic achievements when Magical Spirit visited me again. There were no distractions from the outside world, we were in my bedroom chatting to each other and Magical Spirit shared that there is more you can do for athletics than just run your own race.

I looked at Magical Spirit and asked "What do you mean?" "What else can I do that could also win an event?" I had run hard to win, I had run my own event and I had set some levels of records for some of these events, what I did not know was that there was a way for a team event to be a success as well. Magical Spirit shared that all those girls that are in the same age group as me, that we all have a race together to see who comes in first second, third and fourth, and this then becomes the basis of your relay team. "A relay team?" I asked? "Yes" said Magical Spirit, you run the last leg, second runs the first leg and third runner runs to you to pass the baton in the relay. "It's actually a lot of fun" said Magical Spirit, "I'm sure you will see this occur in the coming days." I then asked Magical Spirit how he knew that I was going to see this this happen. "How is it you always give me an indication of the events as they occur?", I asked. Magical Spirit shared that it was just something he sensed was coming to me and I was being guided to be ready. It's amazing the times you have shared something with me and I have witnessed it occurring, and for that I am grateful, I replied. Magical Spirit looked at me and said, "It's all I see. It is a thought that crosses your mind and you have a very enquiring mind to want to know more so I magically appear every time you seek another answer. You are close to your senior years in school and you have athletics as a curriculum class, I am sure you will witness this very soon.

What occurred to me was that relay events were events that influenced me as well during my senior years at high school. My understanding of getting the first place did have its impact from how fast the other competitors run and this was either a win or a loss of an event. My high school team was fast and we did have some competition in inter-regional school athletic carnivals. Magical Spirit's words were always accurate, he always guided me when I needed it the most and he was always there when I felt unsure.

- ʃ -

Whatever area of the track you were on had an impact on the start of your event. How well you got away from the blocks was the indicator as to how good your race was, and relay races were no different. I would visualise myself winning my event, however, I also had to depend on 3 others to get me there in the 4 x 100 meter relays. This was a different process as you had about 20 feet to pass the baton over from team member to team member and if dropped it was a sure sign that you have massive ground to catch up. To add to the difficulty of the challenge, if you stepped out of the allocated change over square your team stood the chance of being disqualified. In relay events this took skill and concentration to get the baton and can be in full speed when that occurred.

One of the hardest things is to judge the speed of the competitor coming to you with the baton, because if you started too soon you would run out of space to hand over and this would have your team disqualified from the competition. Dropping the baton also had a huge impact on the team as well, especially in the last leg of the race. I recall a time when this happened and it really did put us behind in the catch up, nevertheless, we did make it to the end though outside of the medal contentions.

The baton changing was a crucial element of relay racing and getting the baton into your hand at the right moment made or broke the overall race. As I type now I can visualise the moment the baton reached my hand and I can also hear the noise of the whistle it made as I swung my arm through the wind. I can also connect to the adrenaline that occurred waiting for that baton to reach my hand. Being so connected to noises, feelings and visualising is what makes us want to move forward in our dreams. Imagine what it would be like if you had the feelings and visualise what your dreams are. Imagination is the key.

Sit still and quiet, visualise, imagine what your results are, picture yourself achieving your dreams.

Remember when you were at high school, everyone stepped onto the athletic track and had to compete in a sporting team event or for competition sport. See yourself and visualise for a moment, your team buddy is running to you and you see them approaching fast, however, there is one problem, she has the baton in the opposite hand to the way you wish to take the baton, what would you do? This happened to me.

Quick thinking at the time had me change hands, move to the other side of the track so that I can run together with her to get the baton. Conversely, I could just move and trust that she will deliver to my hand. This occurred to me in a crucial event, we had a last minute, change of runners due to the competition on the day and this changed all our practice efforts. The person I thought I would be getting the baton from was now running second so the second runner was now in the third leg. She was right handed. I had to change my normal right hand to be my left hand and this led to a small concern about a possible dropping of baton as I would normally run with the baton in my right hand. I took the baton in the left hand and held it tight. It wasn't about to leave my hand and I ran hard to the finish line. It was at the end of the line I realised where the baton was and swapped it over, there was now no chance of dropping it after the race was run and won.

With a team effort, we all stood gallantly on the dais, we had finished second representing our school in the Regional Athletic Carnival.

Whilst in the arena of Little Athletics most of my events were solo; I competed against others. However, I cannot recall any team events as I experienced in the school arena. These team events were the 4 x 100 meters' relays. I was always the last runner because of my speed and ability to catch others as I merged through the field.

In a team event, we all must work together. One of the things that I learnt here was that everyone had to do their best, that was how the team would win. I still had to perform my best as well. Sometimes my team would be out in front of the other competitors for the first two legs and the third leg would slow us down. I was always sure to accept the baton at the change firmly. I really loved to hear the wind whistle as I moved the baton through the air to the end. I loved that sound, it urged me on. Sometimes in a race the 3rd runner would lose position and would come from behind me for the baton change, this made it harder to catch up on the passing competitors. Nevertheless, I knew I had that power to move towards the finish line in a good place.

My mindset was very strong in team events as I knew it would be hard to be at the top all the time. I knew what I wanted for myself, however, I had no control on the others in the team. Nothing I did could make them want to win or go faster, they had to want that for themselves and collectively it would all come together for the race. I always kept my focus on winning the event. However, not all were as strong as I was in their athletic ability and most other schools also had weak legs at some point. The weakest leg would sometimes run first or second, and in our team, they normally run third. The strategy was to get out in front, and then have a strong leg to complete the final 100meters. Sometimes this would work, at other times it did not. However, we did make it to the top most of the times in the school sports arena.

Wouldn't it be amazing if you could be a champion at your specialist event? This will appeal to some and to others it won't. That's ok. Whatever that goal is for you, wouldn't it be amazing if you could see yourself achieving it?

అనుఅ

Pearls of Wisdom

☺ The overall lesson here was to always be in control of your own thoughts and strengths. Nobody can tell you what to do, they may give you guidance and encouragement - i.e. like a coach or a personal trainer.
The result is in your strength and the abilities you have.

Everything you need -

comes from within

Chapter 11

CROSSING THE FINISH LINE

I had been taught to run the race to win and be very happy with wherever I finished in the end results. Sometimes that would-be a forth or even a fifth, depending on the competition and the overall race. I learnt this at a very early age and when I connected it with my own ability to run fast I always wanted to cross the finish line first. I had the opportunity to coach a young eleven-year old girl in athletics not long after I was retired from the work force. During one of the training sessions I noticed that she did not run through the finish line as we trained. When I questioned her reason for this I was surprised that she had given up before she had reached the finish line, and only took the step over it. Thus, her race was done so much earlier in the race instead of finishing the race past the finish line. Her result was amazing when she realised where the finish line was and how to run through it till the end.

I can recall that running past the finish line was what gave me that edge to be in front all the time. I wanted that finish line to be there for me to cross it and then finish the race past the finish line. I know I did do this as mentioned in a previous chapter. I finished anything up to 50 meters past the line, I was going so fast. When I realised what was happening to the young girl I was training we then concentrated on the line past the finish, it was then her events and times improved. She started to go faster as she ran past the finish line. I saw such an improvement in her.

One of my suggestions was to have her only look at the car or the tree or whatever was her main line of sight and tell her to run fast to this. She would gauge when she had crossed the line and this would have an impact on her event. It's amazing the improvement in herself and her style since we corrected this. Running to the line is not the race; running past the line is what wins the race. If you are running at your best, you are in top speed as you cross the line and there is no point stopping before. There is no point just making a mark at the line, it's the follow through that wins the event.

Imagine what it would be like to see the line in front of you, you slow down before the line only to step over it. Your time would have slowed down, your momentum was slowing and you were not at top speed. If you can see the finish line in any race, always have momentum that you are in top speed till you cross that finish line. See yourself achieving crossing the finish line for your event in your mind. You will always be at your best when this is done.

As I positioned myself in the crouch position at the start of any race, I would visualise myself crossing the finish line so I already had a view of how fast I had to be going even to get to that point. I knew in me that the finish line was a marker, not the end. It was going past the finish line that at the end was my aim. When I first started athletic sports, and running in lanes marked with string I recall crossing the finish line with a light tape around the waist, this was an indication that you were the winner as I would break the tape and it would flow on behind me. The officials would come and take my arm and move me to the place for first and give me a ticket with the time on it. The official's role was to replace the tape back into position for the next competitor to come through. It was a good indicator who was the winner.

From the twine lined events in the school ground to moving to the Little Athletic arena, we had to run inside the lime line mark on the ground. There was no string to guide you. The only thing the lime marked on the ground was good for was that if you ran on the line it would mark the ground and your feet and this would show possible disqualification, something that would have you taken out of the race results.

When the official raised the red flag, it was not a good sign for that particular lane. I come close a couple of times with the lanes next to me being disqualified, However, I don't recall being disqualified myself. I was so aware of staying in the middle of the lane.

You know what's funny is that you see the lines of the lane and you think you are in the middle of the lane, yet from the official observer you could be so close to the line that can cause for one to be disqualified. Whenever I ran the 200 meters it was always a thing I really had to think about as I rounded the bend, it was a natural drive to be close to the line as you rounded the bend into the straight. I can recall working on this race with some strategies so that I ran in the middle of the lane. Things that come to mind were use the bend to build up speed and watch the middle of the lane to guide you and then line up the middle of the track once you hit the 100 meter straight and aim for the finish line.

Whether it was a team event or a solo event, the main aim of any race is about crossing the finish line, preferably in first position. However, at some point you may cross the line in 6th position, this is ok as well; it's more about crossing the line at full speed.

Interesting as it may seem, as a young child I liked to be the one with the tape around me from the school sports event. That really had a good feeling to it. You knew you were number one as the official would hold your arm he/she would grab the next person and so on down to the end of the competitors then you had to move to the marshal's tent and tell them your name and another official would be close by to call out the time for the event. This was when you received your ticket for the race. It was that ticket that you kept with you and pasted in a book for your indications of progress. Some kids didn't do this, I know I did and still have those ticket books today.

Crossing the line was the best feeling to have when you knew you had run hard to do the best you could. When you had your ticket with the indication of your time on it; it gave a good feeling to know you did it in a good time. I know there was often a comparison of race times with other competitors when the results were registered from the heats for the finals and you could see who you were running against in the semi-finals or finals.

The vision of the finish line was of such importance to me when I ran. I would see past this imaginary line and aim for a point beyond the line. My focus was strong to stay with my vision forward all the time.

Did I look to the left or right during the race? Yes, sometimes I did. However, for the majority of times I was only focused on the result. Looking to the left or right or even over your shoulder could result in losing inches of momentum and a small lack of concentration that could cost you the race. I remember hearing of someone who looked over their shoulder to check and lost momentum and finished second in the race. Now we do see long distance runners always looking to see where the bulk of competitors are in their race, however it is a different strategy of a race. As a sprinter, the focus must be the finish line as '100 metres;' was over in 13 seconds or under and that did not leave a lot of time for correction.

The finish line represented lots of good things. It was the completion to a heat, semi-final and the final of the race. It was an indicator that you had competed and it was a huge credit to your achievement that you had succeeded in the event. That was something that I felt inside of me; being proud I had done it. Reaching first place was the highest feeling of pride I could feel. It was a huge feeling inside, maybe never shown on the outside, However, nevertheless, I felt a deep joy from winning.

At the end of each race it was always most important to come back and shake hands with the other competitors who you ran against and congratulate them on their efforts. Something I learnt very early in life was to always make the effort to congratulate the winner or other place getters on their achievements. It's what a good sportsman does. There were times when I was not first so this was a good practice to get into.

Crossing the finish line in a final's event is really an exhilarating experience, you can't go too far as the officials want the 3 place-getters to stay close so that medal presentations can be made. In some cases, we had to go and sit with other officials and wait for the medals to be scribed and then we were called to the podium.

Sometimes you could take your spikes/shoes off before you were presented on the podium and other times you didn't have enough time to do that.

The presentation of the medals was always a huge impact, especially if you were one of the top 3. I made it to this level several times in my athletic career and I am so proud of my achievements to have received a gold and silver medal. To have your name called out over the microphone and speakers around the ground also brought a tear of joy to my soul. It was a great effort to be standing there and being recognised for the placement on the dais.

Now it's your turn to believe in your dream that you will achieve. What do you want to achieve for yourself? What do you believe is possible for your goal?

ॐॐॐ

Pearls of Wisdom

☺ Visualise it; believe it and focus on it to be your success.

Chapter 12

WHO IS MAGICAL SPIRIT?

Who is magical spirit?

Have you worked out what this is?

It's always with you in everything you do.

Every one of us has a Magical Spirit. For some it is hidden and for others it's alive and connected… nobody is right nor wrong, it is just what it is in life.

Your own intuition; your 3rd eye perception, is also aligned to Magical Spirit. You may also hear a voice chatter in your head, or sometimes you may talk to yourself – this too is Magical Spirit.

Your imagination can bring it alive, -

IT IS IN ALL OF US.

It was my intention to have you consider the spiritual side of life and tap into that magnificent power we each hold within. It's your soul identity. It's a voice that seems to come from another part of you; you can't see touch or smell it, there is no physical sound - it's the chatter inside our head. It's the voice we hear when we are talking to ourselves, expecting an answer back. The connection to this can also be known as Universe, others can refer to it as GOD, whichever sits right for you is what is right. Nobody else can claim that, nobody else has the right too.

It's a source of energy that vibrates and is everywhere in the universe, it's a source of energy that sometimes feels negative when you are under some pressure. It's a source of energy that is around you when you feel on top of the world and are happy. It is an invisible source that is inside each of us and most of us are yet to discover.

I connected to this energy at a very young age. I just did not know what it was. It took many years and different pathways for me to really appreciate and come to understand what was happening. The subject is not taught in schools because it has many variances to it. Different understanding for each culture is also accepted. What I have endeavoured to do is share with you in this book what has been true experiences that I have witnessed in my young childhood days which I am now happy to share with others. Energetically we have all witnessed things around us change and being in connection with your pure essence, your soul, and your magic spiritual guide is the best anyone could ever ask for in life.

To be spiritual you must have the faith and belief in your dreams. You must believe that it is achievable. It may appear invisible; However, it is achievable when you align all your sources together.

VISUALISE - GOAL

- ACTION - ACHIEVE

Deepak Chopra who was an inspiration for me to write my book shares a story on page 14-15 of his "Fire in the Heart" book that is a brilliant example of tasting something that is totally invisible:

"To be spiritual you have to believe in something invisible. First you have to stop trusting that only your five senses are right. It's a hard habit to break, because common sense says, I want to see it, touch it, taste it – then I'll know it's real". However, I can make you taste something right now that is totally invisible.

"Close your eyes and see a bright yellow lemon in your mind's eye. Now see a knife cutting the lemon into slices, and then see yourself biting into one slice.

Did you notice that your mouth started watering? This happened exactly as if you were biting into the lemon. All it took was a mental picture, which you produced out of nowhere and suddenly your body went into action. Millions of cells in our brain formed the image, a signal was sent along the network of nerves inside your head to your mouth;

your saliva glands received the message and began to flow.

Here are the amazing facts that follow from this simple experiment:

There was no picture of a lemon inside your head, when you thought of a lemon your brain cells didn't paint an image or project one on a screen, your brain is as dark as the darkest cave, there's no light or colour inside it. So where did that picture come from?

There was no taste of lemon in your mouth. You didn't actually experience real lemon juice. Your salivary glands, which you may think need food to react to, here needed nothing at all.

So where did the sourness come from?

Some place mysterious.

Let the lemon be your goal or dream,

Let the experience you want to have.

Be the knife cutting the lemon and

Let the achievement of the goal

Be the tasting of the lemon in

your mind's eye.

It's not there in the physical, however,

it's real for you in your mind.

Take lots of steps in the right direction -

and GO FOR IT!!

Author, Intuitive Awareness Coach, Speaker

(The Well Used Key- The Keys to Unlock Your Inner Potential)

Jan Muir

ABOUT THE AUTHOR

Jan, lead a relatively quiet life until she faced a few of life's adversities. She gained her true strength to fight and keep the dream alive. She first achieved to her credit as a young ten year old to reach state championships in Athletics with a gold medal. It was her athletic pathway that she showed great potential. Dreams, goals of reaching more gold were gone, in one split second - for the mind to conceive. It only took a family members comment to shatter her dreams and she never run again.

Jan has witnessed and experienced many life changing events. In 1998 she faced losing her partner of 30 odd years to the disease Alzheimer's Dementia. Year 2000 she placed him in a home. In late 2001 uplifted from Darwin moved to Brisbane; in 2002 partner passed away. In 2003 her daughter moved back to Darwin to start a fresh life and now happily married with 2 children. In 2005 diagnosed with pre cervical cancer and gets all clear - it was caught in time.

6 short months later Jan was diagnosed in 2006 with breast cancer and faced radical surgery to have to fight to keep the dream alive again. In 2007 after 9 months away from

employment Jan faces the gradual return to work from then onwards to 2011 she faced her personal challenges of development and growth after her illness. During this time, she wrote lots of notes on parts of her life as a way of coping during a challenging time in life. It wasn't until around 2009 Jan had the chance to study Think and Grow Rich by Napoleon Hill and then it finally clicked Jan started to write of her experiences and bring this into a book.

With another adversity in 2012 Jan faced being retrenched from her long career in the Public Service after having been employed for over 30 years.

Jan self-published her first book in late 2012 and 2015 her second edition was re-published with guidance and enhanced new content. This has led her on a path of new discovery to want to write more.

Jan currently has another 5 books on the go with her publishing team all falling into place. Her inspiration is mainly to inspire the young adult to see themselves already achieving what they desire in life; and is adaptable to be applied to anyone in life. This books Vision to WIN is a story about Jan's athletic days, and the journey of her life and what she learnt along the way.

How to win Gold all using the power of the mind.

Please feel free to jot down anything that comes to mind as your read….. Keep this as your journal pages   ENJOY

Run the dream of your life